Lads, You're Wanted

Hambleden and the Great War

Chris Whitehead

Ken Cugnoni
Charles Hussey

Birch Cottage Publications
Pheasants' Hill
Hambleden
RG9 6SN

Email: WW1_Hambleden@outlook.com

ISBN 978-1-915292-05-6

Produced by Biddles Ltd. King's Lynn, Norfolk PE32 1SF

This book is dedicated to the memory of all the men and women
from Hambleden, Frieth and Skirmett
who suffered in the Great War.

Photographic consultant Sally Hedges Greenwood ARPS
Map of Hambleden © Old Maps and Ordnance Survey.
Photograph of Rose Cottage and Yew Tree Inn, Frieth courtesy of
'Joan Barksfield's Collection' http://www.friethhistory.org
Photographs of Hambleden Centre and Hambleden Church courtesy
of Barry Eastick.
Photograph of Greenlands, Workers in Field & WI Float courtesy of
Jim Cleary.

The photographs of individual soldiers are mainly taken from
microfilm copies of the South Bucks Press and are consequently of
poor quality, for which we apologise.

Contents

Introduction

They went with songs to the battle, they were young,
Straight of limb, true of eye, steady and aglow.
They were staunch to the end against odds uncounted,
They fell with their faces to the foe.

They shall grow not old, as we that are left grow old:
Age shall not weary them, nor the years condemn.
At the going down of the sun and in the morning
We will remember them.

From 'For The Fallen' by Laurence Binyon

By 1920 over 5,000 war memorials had been constructed across the land to commemorate the fallen of the Great War. In Hambleden, ours was erected on land that had previously been a vegetable garden. As only two of our war dead have graves in the Parish, the Memorial is the nearest that many of the relatives would come to having a grave for their loved ones.

Forty-six names are on our War Memorial, in the Roll of Honour in our Churches, or on the Memorial Board in our Village Hall. Yes, forty-six! Even allowing for the fact that some did not live in Hambleden in 1914, and some, frankly, seem to have had no links with Hambleden at all – that is a huge number from the 190 men (and one woman) from our tiny parish of Hambleden, Frieth and Skirmett (hereafter, for the sake of brevity, simply referred to as Hambleden) who joined up. Just stop for a minute.............and think how we would feel if we lost forty-six of the young men of Hambleden today, say, in some sort of natural disaster, with no

1

bodies to recover and bury. It is too horrible to contemplate. Well, their loved ones would have felt exactly the same way - they too were all sons, brothers, lovers, husbands and fathers. It must have been devastating.

Even talking about 'the forty-six' reduces these men to an abstract statistic. They are not a statistic – they lived, they existed. Each man whose name is commemorated was an individual. The people of 1914 were fully human, not crude abstractions to be lost in the big picture. So, with the centenary of the outbreak of the Great War in August, I thought it might be a fitting tribute to the Hambleden men that died to try to reconstruct the people behind the names – who they were, what regiment they were in, how old were they, where they lived, what they did for a living; and also to explore the experience of what it was like to live in Hambleden in the years and months leading up to the War. In other words, what was Hambleden like in 1914?

I have not set out to draw political conclusions, though it is difficult not to do so when writing about war. I have also been mindful not to be too sombre, though that too is difficult when writing about war and death. In attempting to understand why the population seemed readily to consent to war, I have tried to get away from the generalisation of war enthusiasm, though I do not deny that the majority reaction to the war was patriotic and in some respects idealistic ('the war to end all wars'). Some commentators have suggested that men were fighting because of an 'unwavering commitment to defending peace and freedom', or that they were defending 'the western liberal international order'. I doubt soldiers at the time would have put it like that, though no doubt they felt distinctive by freely fighting for the freedom of others. However, if asked they would have told you, more prosaically, that they were fighting for their country, and their own families and friends. They believed, rightly or wrongly, and to varying degrees, their choice was between war and the German domination of Europe – and that such domination would be a disaster.

Throughout these pages, I have referred to the war as the Great War, which of course it was at the time. It was not until 1939 that it became the First World War. I hope this makes the story seem more contemporary than historical; hindsight carries risks when applied to understanding the thoughts and actions of people in the past – it is unavailable to them, and they do not have its luxury to inform their decisions.

I have tried not to attribute ideas and motives retrospectively in order to suit my own beliefs – one person's myth is another one's incontrovertible truth. Either the generals were all donkeys or they were sensible men doing their best. The war was either a colossal mistake or a struggle for important principles. Such polarisation may make for a good spectacle but it does not do what history should – and that is to help us to understand the past in all its complexity. Our understanding is not helped either by the detachment of the War from its historical moorings into popular fiction – even by serious authors such as Pat Barker and Sebastian Faulks - and into the canonical poetry of the War Poets. Great literature it may be, but not necessarily good history.

Perhaps the first thing to understand about the decade before the outbreak of war is that, even in Hambleden, society contained not one, but several, worlds, from the hugely wealthy Smiths living in Greenlands to the agricultural labourer living in four rooms with his six children.

For us, a hundred years on, perhaps the most difficult imaginative leap is to comprehend the world of the working class – into which the majority of the forty-six were born. No view of the horrors of the Great War can be complete without a sense of the horrors of the pre-war peace – I have tried to describe them in the chapter on Hambleden. The rawness of life prior to 1914 gave capacities for endurance on the part of soldiers and civilians alike which are now hard to imagine.

Nevertheless, tough as it was, it was a way of life that people were prepared to make sacrifices to defend, for it was felt to have been an improvement on what had gone before - bad as living conditions were in 1914, they were better for most people than they had been for their parents and grandparents. Even those with little to lose did not want to lose what little they had, and when tales of German atrocities in Belgium filtered through, there was a determination for it not to happen here. What the Great War meant in people's lives was to a certain degree conditioned by these pre-war situations. Moreover, as wages rose between 1914 and 1918, it is fair to say that the overall effect of the War, with all qualifications acknowledged, is that the poor became less poor. In some cases, this shakes the foundations of the myth of the war as a universal catastrophe.

Strange as it may seem, even the Army, even the horrors of the Western Front could seem in some respects an improvement on day-to-day civilian life. Many, perhaps most, soldiers were better fed in the Army than they had ever been - to eat meat every day was a genuine novelty, even if it was only bully beef. The lack of privacy and decency, which was felt so deeply by middle-class men in the forces, despite the experiences of the dormitories and changing rooms of their public schools, was no stranger to many working class soldiers. Army life included a great deal of hard monotonous labour – they were used to that – but for many men it also included more genuine leisure than they had ever previously experienced. Even the fear of death or maiming should be seen in a pre - war context.

Of course, this is neither to deny nor belittle in any way the traumatic experiences of battle, the oppressive nature of army discipline and the discomfort of outdoor living in sordid conditions (everyone hated mud, even those used to it), and above all the emotional burden of separation from family (home leave was every fourteen months, on average). On the whole, Army service was a grim experience. Nevertheless, it is reasonable to suggest that many of the soldiers from Hambleden found their experiences less shocking and unusual than might be expected.

In 2014, as we begin to mark the centenary of the Great War, my intention in writing these notes is most certainly to honour those who died, and to do so with gratitude, but not to glorify. To tell their story is the only way we have left to remember, and the only way to pass it on. And it is important to pass it on, important for the men who died and for those who suffered long afterwards and grieved all their lives. They are part of the unique chemistry that makes our parish the place we love. And important for us too. If they gave their todays for our tomorrows, then, I am sure, after all they went through, and died for, they would wish to see us doing all we can to create a world of peace and goodwill. Yes, to be determined to guard our freedom, but as far as humanly possible, to do it in peace.

This book is in three chapters; at the end is a page for each one of the forty-six. I have tried to trace them all through various websites and elsewhere with varying degrees of success. Although we may never know how some names came to be commemorated in our village, others are still familiar to us – Dawson, Gray, Plumridge, Tilbury. Time and·resources have restricted me to researching only three of the names in detail, but I believe they are representative, and provide an insight into what Hambleden was like in 1914.

The first chapter attempts to set some context – what was the world like in 1914; what was going on that would have amused, interested and intrigued the people in Hambleden. When setting out on this project I had only a sketchy knowledge of the background to the outbreak of war in 1914 – more though than Baldrick, famously in Blackadder *'it started when a bloke called Archie Duke shot an ostrich 'cause he was hungry'!* So, on the assumption that there may be one or two more like me, whose knowledge is somewhere between Baldrick and reality, I have also included a few paragraphs on how the war came about.

Chapter 2 looks in more detail at some of the specifics of life in Hambleden at the time: the working life, the employers, housing conditions, and what ordinary folk did for leisure. What is so striking now, a century later, is the wonderful humanity of the people, their humour, their sense of fun and their capacity for hard work.

Chapter 3 looks at the forty-six, why they went to fight, and the lives and deaths of three of them in particular. I hope you will come to know them as well as I feel I have. I attempt to examine the motives behind their enlistment, look at the role of the Church, the shambles of basic training, and what life in the Army was like for them.

Finally, there is a profile of each man collating all the information we could gather. There are many gaps – indeed, there are three men for whom we can find no information at all - which perhaps will be filled over the next few years by relations and friends of relations that knew of the men. Every day new books and sources of information are published – for example, the Imperial War Museum has recently launched a website featuring millions of photos, letters and diaries of those who took part in the war effort. No doubt, these will also fill some of the gaps.

For currency conversions, multiply 1914 values by 100, and you won't be far out when comparing to today's price levels.

I have refrained from giving in detail the authority for every statement, as I believe the effect would be more bewildering than helpful for the ordinary reader for whom this book is intended. However, a list of the principal sources is included at the end.

Although my name is on the cover, this has been a joint effort with Ken Cugnoni and Charles Hussey. Charles did most of the research on the individual men; Ken corrected my grammar, and spotted the typos that 'Spellcheck' missed. We have tried to verify all our facts, though this was difficult from time to time as there are often inconsistencies between sources, for example to do with names and dates. We jointly assume responsibility for the errors, of which there will probably be many; we are bound to have left something out or got something wrong. We will put these right in a second edition, for surely there will be need of one – perhaps to coincide with the Armistice.

Naturally, we apologise if inadvertently we have trodden on some personal sensitivities.

We thank the Rector, John Wigram for allowing us access to the Parish Magazines of the time, which have revealed a world both significantly different and yet totally recognisable to the Hambleden of today. Thanks also to Mrs Jill Wennberg who has given us access to the school headmaster's Log; thankfully, education of village children has changed beyond measure over the past century!

Any profits from the sale of this book are going to Hambleden Village Hall, which up to 1897 was the village school in which most of the forty-six started their education. Because of the charitable nature of the project, we beg forgiveness if we have unintentionally infringed any copyright.

Chris Whitehead
Pheasants' Hill
14 May 2014

Setting the Scene

We are the Dead. Short days ago
We lived, felt dawn, saw sunset glow,
Loved and were loved, and now we lie
In Flanders fields.

From 'In Flanders Fields' by John McCrae

The Great War still casts its shadows both physically and in our imaginations. Tons of ordnance are still buried in the battlefields and every so often someone - an unlucky farmer ploughing in Belgium, perhaps - is added to the casualty lists. Indeed, as I write these notes on 19 March 2014, I hear that two Belgian workmen have been killed by an unexploded shell which was dug up on a building site in Ypres. Every spring after the ground has unfrozen, units of Belgian and French armies have to gather up the unexploded shells that have been heaved up. Scrawled across the plains of Picardy and Flanders, even after a century, are the traces of old trench lines. Here and there, a thicket of nettles marks the entrance to a long-sealed tunnel or hints at a deep dugout buried in the earth below. In our memories the Great War, thanks in part to an extraordinary outpouring of memoirs and novels and paintings, but also because so many of us have long forgotten family connections to it, remains a dark and dreadful chapter in our history. My own grandfather was in the Royal Navy. His ship HMS Kennet was stationed off the coast of China at Tsingtao, blockading the German base there. On 22 August 1914 she was damaged in action with a German torpedo boat, a German gunboat and a 4-inch shore battery. My grandfather, then 21 years old, was severely injured and was hospitalised. His family did not hear of him or from him for over a year, and were most surprised when he finally turned up on their doorstep. Family legend has it that he was the first sailor to be wounded in the Great War (incorrectly, as it turns out!) - which as we can see, even after less than three weeks, had become truly a global conflict.

Not only is ordinance regularly discovered, but so also are bodies. The corpses of ten soldiers that had been discovered back in 2009 during construction work near the French village of Beaucamps-Ligny have recently been identified as members of the York and Lancaster Regiment after DNA analysis of samples from relatives. And in one of the strangest consequences of global warming, glaciers in the Italian Alps are slowly melting to reveal the frozen corpses of soldiers killed during the War. The bones of three Hapsburg soldiers, complete with the tattered remains of their uniforms and personal effects, have recently been revealed. And so it goes on..........

The conflict that began in the summer of 1914 mobilised 65 million troops, claimed three empires, 20 million military and civilian deaths, and 21 million wounded. Memorials tell us of the dead. Less regarded are the disfigured, the men who lost noses, mouths, jaws and sometimes almost whole faces and who lived on, in Jeremy Paxman's phrase, as 'walking gargoyles', and the millions who suffered psychological trauma, who repressed their worst memories on their return from the front and would not confront nor discuss them, often with appalling psychological results. Their experiences sometimes only resurfaced in nightmares - the condition of post-traumatic stress disorder was not officially recognised as a mental health condition until 1980. This commemoration is for them as well. Of those that died, forty-six came from or were associated with Hambleden, hereafter referred to as 'Our Men'. Among all the statistics, it is easy to overlook the fact that all the casualties were real people, with families, homes and jobs. This small commemoration seeks not only to discover who Our Men were, but also to attempt to describe the Hambleden of 1914, and identify the influences that caused them to leave the tranquillity of our valley for the horrors of war. Like most men of their background, they had almost certainly never been abroad before they travelled to their deaths on the battlefields of Europe. Their names are recorded on our War Memorial, in our Churches and in our Village Hall, and in the sense that we live in the houses that they lived in, look out on the hills that they looked out on, have recently experienced the lethality of Balkan nationalism ourselves and have witnessed the consequences arising from terrorist attacks and suicide bombers, these men are our contemporaries.

They are:

William Barlow	Thomas Gearing	Arthur Richardson
Cecil Batchelor	George Gray	Frederick Rixon
Ernest Batchelor	Harry Gray	Alfred Rose
Sidney Bond	Edmund Higgins	Henry Sherlock
Wilfred Bond	John Holland	Harry Silvester
Charles Buckell	Bertram Honeysett	Valentine Silvester
Percy Clinkard	George Hopper	William Smith
Alfred Coker	George Howson	Walter Stainton
William Collison	Frederick Janes	James Taylor
William Cook	Charles Leaver	Ralph Tilbury
George Cutler	Frederick Leaver	Thomas Trendall
Alfred Dawson	Ernest Lyford	Harry Vivian
Frank Deane	James McCarter	Rowland Webster
Arthur Edwards	Arthur Miles	Sidney White
Arthur Gater	Brian Molloy	Reginald Willsher
	Frederick Plumridge	

Most of Our Men were born around 1890, so one of their earliest memories, and one that certainly would have made a large impression on them would have been Queen Victoria's Diamond Jubilee in 1897.

It was the event in which the British Empire reached its climax, when no fewer than eleven colonial Prime Ministers and any number of maharajahs preceded the Queen Empress to a thanksgiving service in St Paul's, where it was said, only the Almighty was superior. Britain had never appeared so powerful. The Diamond Jubilee was marked around the world by events ranging from marching schoolchildren to fireworks to military reviews. It was, said the Spectator, *'as if one roar of acclaim and loyalty were coming up from the whole earth'*. All over Britain, villages and towns celebrated with banquets and balls, and 2,500 bonfires blazed from one end of the country to the other. Churches held special services; a nation rejoiced.

Further celebrations were to follow. Our Men lived through two coronations and the funerals of two monarchs. 28 June 1914, the day of the assassination at Sarajevo, was the anniversary of the coronation of Queen Victoria. Seventy-seven years later, and thirteen years after her death, the accession of the old Queen was still looked on by the British as the curtain raiser to their golden age. Her birthday, 24 May, became known as Empire Day from 1902, and was declared a public holiday. Hambleden would have been decked with flags, and a special service would have been held in the Church. Schoolchildren would salute the union flag and sing patriotic songs and God Save the King. They would hear inspirational speeches and listen to tales of derring-do from across the Empire, stories that included such heroes as Clive of India, Wolfe of Québec and 'Chinese Gordon' of Khartoum. But of course, the real highlight of the day for the children was that they were let out of school early in order to take part in marches, maypole dances, concerts and parties that celebrated the event. Despite the high jinks, the children were left in no doubt as to the object of their celebrations, nor of the links of pride and responsibility which bound the youngest of them to the far-flung countries, islands and continents where the British flag flapped above government offices, barracks and residences as a symbol of Britain's benevolent rule.

Britain in 1914 was an immensely self-confident country, at the pinnacle of its power that had grown and grown for a century; the British people were accustomed to senior status in international affairs and were used to military victories, large and small (the debacle of the Boer War was forgotten). The country commanded the biggest empire in history and dominated world trade; the empire-builder Cecil Rhodes declared that to be born English was to win first prize in the lottery of life – then, as now, it was convenient for

Britain to paint itself as more righteous and more civilised than the people it occupied and fought with. But, unlike today, Europe in the early twentieth century was merely a distraction; Britain had no ambitions there. Its main objective was to ensure a balance of power among other European states so that none was sufficiently powerful to menace its overseas empire.

However, Britain's relative position had been diminishing over time, growing more slowly than other countries while retaining the habits and ideologies of a previous era of industrial pre-eminence. The only area where Britain remained splendidly dominant was in managing the finances of globalisation, and exporting the nation's capital. The City of London's role in world trade was pivotal - all based on the gold standard, the hallmark of international capitalism, guarantor of a global trading system based on fixed exchange rates pegged to gold. Nearly half of the world's foreign direct investment came from Britain … and therein lay the seeds of its relative decline – by investing abroad, the City was denying investment to industry at home. Germany did not have such foreign distractions.

By 1913, after the Edwardian decade, London was rich and it was powerful. It was the conductor of a worldwide empire. It was the biggest city on the face of the earth. Moreover, it was not standing still politically - in 1911 the House of Lords lost its indefinite veto over legislation and any veto at all over money bills. This was a seismic shift - a sign that democracy was overhauling privilege. However, even after successive reform had widened the franchise and had brought new sorts of men into politics, 60% of MPs still came from the landed classes. Indeed, the last prime minister to sit in the House of Lords did so as recently as 1902. These classes also dominated the Church, the armed forces and the civil service, and herein we find another parallel with modern society for as former Prime Minister John Major commented in November 2013 '*In every single sphere of British influence, the upper echelons of power today are held overwhelmingly by the privately educated or the affluent middle class*'. However, what was different in society in 1913, including Hambleden, was the (albeit diminishing) sense of deference by the working classes, to which most of Our Men belonged, to the 'higher' levels of society, and there was acknowledgement, at least among the gentry, that this was the natural order of things. They were among the most admired and envied classes in the world; all over Europe, the upper classes imported English nannies and grooms, wore tartans, and ate marmalade at breakfast.

Perhaps the most striking characteristic of Our Men was their innocence – their blind, even naïve nationalism, and a sense of class-bound order to their lives. They did not quite have our twenty first century suspicion of groups such as politicians, the police, the financial services and the press. They believed in honour, integrity and a sense of duty - the disregard of individual concerns for a greater good.

However, Our Men would have been well aware that not all was completely rosy in their self-confident Britain. The nature of the country was changing – a change in the locus of power from north to south, and from land and manufacturing to retail and financial services. Domestic pressures were increasing – a rising labour movement, demands for votes for women and for independence of subject nations. Although they would have been no strangers to the use of militancy to achieve political aims (British history is littered with it), they may have been disturbed by events in the early twentieth century which seemed to challenge the stability and even the security of the country.

The Irish Home Rule Bill had been rumbling on for years and finally came to a head in 1913 – no doubt to the total indifference of the good folk of Hambleden. However, I suspect that they may have been more troubled by the wave of industrial strife between 1910 and 1914 – the so-called Great Unrest. Strikes in the docks, the mines and the railways must have affected their lives to some extent – and even a cursory eyebrow may have been raised when mass picketing action at Llanelli railway station was brutally suppressed, resulting in two men being shot dead. Rioting followed; magistrates' homes were attacked and railway trucks were set on fire, resulting in an explosion which killed a further four people.

But the events that would have had the tongues wagging in the Stag and elsewhere were those concerned with securing votes for women. Since 1884 all men paying an annual rental of £10 or all those holding land valued at £10 had the vote. However, suffrage was not universal: although the size of the electorate had been widened considerably, all women and 40% of adult males were still without the vote.

By 1913 Britain had, in effect, been engaged in civil conflict over votes for women for a decade or more. Families and political parties were divided. Common civility had been tested. The conflict had claimed victims and created martyrs. Not only was civil disobedience evident in London, but suffragettes were out in force at the Henley Regatta of 1913 – only three weeks after Emily Davidson had died under the King's horse at the Derby – so Hambleden would have been well aware of the movement. We perhaps will never know how the village divided, but there is no doubt that after the war the culmination of the suffragette movement together with the awareness of the work done by women during the War in the place of the men who were fighting, changed the role of women in society forever.

In short, huge political and social forces were shaking Britain. The country seemed to be menaced by revolution, and its domestic strife made a powerful impression on opinion abroad; a great democracy was seen to be declining into decadence and decay. Britain's allies, France and Russia, were dismayed. Its prospective enemies found it hard to believe that a country convulsed in such a fashion could threaten their continental power and ambitions.

We flatter ourselves to believe we live amid a period of unprecedentedly rapid change. Yet between 1900 and 1914, a similar timeframe to that which divides today from the 2001 terrorist assaults on the United States, technological, social and political advances swept the world on a scale unknown in any previous timespan. Einstein promulgated his theory of relativity, Marie Curie isolated radium, and Leo Baekeland invented Bakelite, the first synthetic polymer. Telephones, gramophones, motor vehicles, cinema performances and electrified homes became commonplace among affluent people.

In Britain, the period was infamous for disasters and loss of life, primarily the loss of the Titanic in 1912 and the Empress of Ireland in 1914, in which more passengers were lost than on the Titanic.

In 1906 the Workmen's Compensation Act provided

compensation for industrial injuries or disease, which was just as well, as the decade was a litany of industrial disasters, mostly in the mining industry: 120 were killed in 1905 in the Rhondda valley; 160 were killed in the Durham accident of 1906; 136 died at the Whitehaven colliery in 1910. Later that year a massive underground explosion at Westhoughton in Lancashire killed 344 men, an enormous number – but superseded in in 1913 by Britain's worst pit disaster when 439 miners died at Senghenydd in South Wales.

The railways too had their share of accidents as the various companies competed to achieve the fastest journey times. In 1906, accidents at Salisbury and Grantham occurred within three months of each other, claiming forty-two lives. Another eighteen lives were lost at Shrewsbury the following year. Closer to home, an accident occurred at Reading on 17 June 1914 when the driver of a train to Ascot moved off even though the signal was at 'danger', and into the path of an oncoming train bound for London Paddington; the only fatality was the driver of the Paddington train.

Notorious crimes kept the country entranced during the decade. In July 1910, Dr Crippen was arrested on board SS Montrose for the murder of his wife after a telegraph was sent to the ship's captain. Within four months, he had been tried and executed. Later that year in Houndsditch, London, a group of Latvian anarchists shot three policemen in a botched raid on a jewellers — three were arrested but other members of the gang escaped, only to be cornered in what became known as the Siege of Sidney Street during which the Metropolitan Police and the Scots Guards engaged in a shootout. It ended with the deaths of two members of the gang. However, perhaps the case that held the firmest grip on the imaginations of Hambleden was that of the unsolved murder of the boy William Starchfield in early 1914. With the Daily Sketch printing a photograph of the dead boy displayed like a waxen doll on its front page, and no obvious leads, everyone became an amateur sleuth in the hope of solving the crime.

Although Our Men may not have been particularly concerned with works of art, one they might have known about would have been the Mona Lisa, the fame of which was emphasised when it was stolen in August 1911. At the time, the painting was believed to be lost forever, and it was two years before the thief was discovered and it was returned to the Louvre. Another well-known painting may have been the Rokeby Venus, especially after the suffragette Mary Richardson walked into the National Gallery and attacked it with a meat cleaver in March 1914.

New developments in technology would have kept the good folks of Hambleden intrigued. This was the period when the motor car began to capture the public imagination By 1900 the first all-British 4-wheel car had been designed and built by Herbert Austin; in 1901, he started what became Wolseley Motors Limited in Birmingham and the UK's largest car manufacturer until Ford in 1913.

In 1905 the Automobile Association was inaugurated. The London to Brighton horse-drawn parcel post coach made its last run, being replaced by a motor lorry. In 1910 the first double-decker bus entered service, displacing the last horse buses by the end of 1911. About 900 saw service on the Western Front in the War.

The great bulk of the pioneering car producers, many of them from the bicycle industry, got off to a shaky start. Of the 200 British makes of car that had been launched up until 1913, only about 100 of the firms were still in existence at the outbreak of the War. In 1910 total UK vehicle production was 14,000 units. In Hambleden cars would have been scarce, though we know from the 1911 Census that at least three local men described their occupation as 'chauffeur'. It seems probable that the Smiths in Greenlands would have owned one – their garage is still there; we know the Molloy's in Woolleys did, and so did the doctor, for the Parish Magazine of September 1914 records that '*Dr Acland fell as he was getting out of his car, and broke his arm*'.

Driving at that time was not trouble free – in May 1911, the Parish magazine noted '*Mr Coombes' motor car, which should have brought the Reverend Baines up to Frieth for the evening service on 5 April, 'refused the hill', so Mr Clark came to the rescue with his horse and trap*' – to much mirth in the village, I suspect!

In 1913 two events occurred that would revolutionise motoring for the masses in Britain: Henry Ford had built a new factory in Manchester and the 'Bullnose' Morris Oxford 2-seater car went on sale. Other car manufacturers included Humber, Rover, Sunbeam, Vauxhall and Rolls Royce.

In fact Charles Rolls was more famous for his exploits in the field of aviation. In 1910 he became the first man to make a non-stop double crossing of the English Channel by plane, including the first eastbound flight. He was also the first British resident to make the crossing in a British-built plane. Sadly, he was killed in an air crash whilst taking part in an air show in July of the same year.

Hambleden, like the rest of Britain, must have followed developments in aviation with a sense of wonder, if not at the technology then at the speed in which developments took place – in the same way that we followed exploration in space in the 1960s and 70's. Although the Wright brothers had made their first powered flight in 1903, it was not until 1907 that British Army Dirigible No 1, christened Nulli Secundus, the UK's first powered airship, made her first flight, from Farnborough to London. The first British powered fixed wing flight took place a year later, and in the same year the Short brothers founded, in Battersea, the first aircraft manufacturing company in England. In 1909, Louis Blériot astounded the nation by flying a monoplane across the English Channel from Calais to Dover, winning a prize of £1,000 from the Daily Mail. In the same year John Moore-Brabazon flew a circular mile and won another £1,000 prize offered by the Daily Mail. On 4 November 1909, as a joke to prove that pigs could fly, he put a small pig in a waste-paper basket tied to a wing-strut of his aeroplane. This may have been the first live cargo flight by aeroplane!

By mid-1914, aviation in England had reached a new summit of popularity. In April, King George and Queen Mary left Dover on the royal yacht for a state visit to Paris. Trailing them in his monoplane was one Bentfield Hucks in his Blériot monoplane, accompanied by a cameraman who filmed a bird's-eye view of the royal party's arrival in France as the plane hovered over Calais harbour. Hucks immediately flew the film back to England where it was rushed off to be developed. An audience at the Coliseum saw the film at a matinée performance that same afternoon!

But the British aviators that really captured the imagination of the public were Claude Grahame-White and Gustav Hamel

(ironically the son of a German doctor, who numbered King Edward among his patients.)

Grahame-White became a celebrity in England in April 1910 when he competed with the French pilot Louis Paulhan for the £10,000 prize offered by the Daily Mail for the first flight between London and Manchester in under 24 hours. Although Paulhan won the prize, Grahame White's achievement was widely praised.

Three months later he won the £1,000 first prize for Aggregate Duration in Flight (1 hr. 23 min 20 secs) at the Midlands Aviation Meeting at Wolverhampton and the Gordon Bennett Aviation Cup race in Belmont Park, Long Island, New York, for which he was awarded the Gold Medal of the Royal Aero Club.

His most noted achievements though were centred on the commercialisation of aviation, developing Hendon as the centre of British aviation, where he built workshops, flying schools, grandstands, pavilions and a clubhouse. Admission to airshows would set back a spectator between 6d and 10 shillings (£2 - £50 in today's money). Three quarters of a million visitors went to Hendon in 1913, and it was considered a poor gate if 10,000 people were not present.

Supported by Lord Northcliffe and HG Wells, he was instrumental in promoting the military application of air power before the Great War with a campaign called "Wake Up Britain", and experimented with fitting various weapons and bombs to planes. In 1912, The Royal Flying Corps was established, and by the end of 1914 it was clear that aircraft were not only here to stay, but had become a weapon of war when The Royal Navy's first aircraft carrier, HMS Ark Royal, was commissioned.

Hamel's celebrity was partly because he was very well connected through his father, and was a personal friend of the First Lord of the Admiralty, Winston Churchill, an inveterate flier. Because of this touch of stardust, he was immensely popular. In the exploit for which Hamel is best remembered, he flew a Blériot on Saturday 9 September 1911, covering the 21 miles between Hendon and Windsor in 18 minutes to deliver the first official airmail to the Postmaster General. He carried one bag of mail with 300-400 letters, about 800 postcards and a few newspapers. Included in his delivery was a postcard he had written en route.

17

Late in 1913, he perfected looping the loop, which became a popular event during his many public displays. On 2 January 1914, Hamel took a Miss Trehawke Davies aloft to experience a loop, and she thus became the first woman in the world to do so. He disappeared over the English Channel on 23 May 1914 while returning from Paris in a new 80 hp Morane-Saulnier monoplane he had just collected; he was not yet 25.

Things were appearing in the shops that would have made folks lives a little more bearable. The decade saw the first appearance of the following: Aspirin, Bisto, Vimto and Lucozade. From 1909, these products could be bought at Woolworth's. Women were no doubt pleased when Woman's Weekly was launched in 1911; perhaps not so pleased when Carter's Crisps of London introduced potato crisps to an unsuspecting public in 1913, and junk food was born.

In sport, the decade saw the formation of Chelsea Football Club, the first £1,000 football transfer, the emergence of Manchester United as a major footballing force, and the move of Arsenal from Woolwich to Highbury. Incidentally, the Football Association was to come in for severe criticism for not abandoning the 1914-15 season on the outbreak of War.

However, the game which defined the era was cricket. It was, without doubt, the game of empire – to this day at the highest level it is still played only between England and her colonies or former colonies. Cricket, like religion, was one of the building blocks of colonisation; it was considered to have higher levels of sportsmanship than other games, uniquely promoting qualities such as fair play, selflessness, putting the team before the individual, and, perhaps crucially, accepting the decisions of the umpire and captains without complaint, even if they were wrong.

Now, a hundred years on, there is evidence that match fixing has been committed in international and domestic cricket by a mix of players, umpires, and administrators from across the Test-playing nations. More than a hundred individuals around the world are suspected of involvement in fixing, and the ICC, the governing body of world cricket, are about to appoint Indian N Srinivasan as chairman even though he has been suspended by the supreme court of India while investigations are held into his conduct regarding allegations of corruption. All those who were involved in cricket in 1914, from Lord Hawke, President of the MCC to the enthusiastic trundler who turned out occasionally for Hambleden, must be turning in their graves.

Followers of cricket (of which there were many in Hambleden then, as now) were fortunate to witness what has become known as 'the Golden Age' – the twenty summers prior to the War. Cricket boomed at all levels. Village, club and league cricket became ever more popular, and there are several references to it in the Parish Magazines of the day:

July 1903: Hambleden - *'We ask the cricketers, for the sake of the grass, not always to pitch their wickets in the same spot'*

July 1904: Frieth - *'the chief occupations of the village lately have been gardening, hay-making and cricket'.*

June 1912: Frieth – *'the first match at the new ground at Parmoor was played on 18 May.'*

June 1914: Frieth – *'we have played two matches, getting thoroughly beaten in both.'*

After the death of Our Man Sidney Bond in 1915, the South Bucks Press commented that he *'was well-known in Stokenchurch, and also in the Wycombe and District Cricket League circles, as he had assisted Stokenchurch in many of their League fixtures. His services were much sought after, being a good bowler, as well as bat, and many are sorry to hear of his death.'*

Other Men that we know were active cricket players were Edmund Higgins, Arthur Miles, Brian Molloy and Sidney White.

County allegiances were strong, and alternative summer pursuits could not compete with the game's drama. The County Championship was the most important sporting competition in the country; the improvement in literacy and the growth of newspapers meant it could be followed daily by supporters in Hambleden and elsewhere. It was by far the most popular of spectator team sports – about two million watched first class matches in 1910, double that of football.

Not the least curious aspect of this splendid popularity was the role of the amateur. In other countries, and indeed in other pastimes in Britain, it was the norm for the upper crust to relax and to be entertained by paid, usually working class, performers; in cricket, broadly the reverse was the case. The attractions of cricket to gentlemen amateurs were its aristocratic rhythms, taking a huge amount of time interspersed with plenty of breaks for eating, relaxing, drinking and socialising. One of the highlights of the season was the annual Gentlemen (amateur) v Players (professional) match at Lords.

As sport reflects the age, so professionals, although comparatively well paid, were treated shabbily when compared to the amateurs – they had different changing rooms, stayed in worse hotels, and emerged on to the playing field through separate gates. Their names were represented differently on scorecards – amateurs were listed as 'Mr' or 'Esq' with their initials before rather than after their surnames - so that even in 1950, when Fred Titmus played his first game at Lords, an announcement came over the loudspeaker: *'Ladies and gentlemen, a correction to your scorecards: for 'FJ Titmus' please read 'Titmus FJ'.* It was not until 1952 that a professional was appointed as captain of the England team.

The former England captain, Mike Brearley, remembers that, as late as 1960, when as a schoolboy he played for the Middlesex 2nd XI at Hove, he and the captain, R V C Robbins (Esq) *'changed in a large room plush with carpets and sofas. The other ten - all professionals - were changing in a tiny makeshift room virtually under the showers.'*

Be that as it may, the top five English batsmen of all time played in the decade leading up to the War – professionals Jack Hobbs, Frank Woolley, Patsy Hendron and Charles Mead, and WG Grace, who symbolised and promoted the concept of the gentleman amateur while at the same time pocketing large match fees. He retired in 1908 and it was to him that the huge popularity of cricket in the early twentieth century was attributed. When he died in 1915, the Manchester Guardian wrote of him:

> *'Dr. William Gilbert Grace was by common consent the greatest and most attractive figure that ever appeared on the cricket field. In his all-round mastery of the game, in the length of years during which he stood far above all rivals, in the amazing sum total of his cricketing achievements, and, by no means least of all in the popular interest he excited, no*

cricketer, living or dead, has ever approached him, and it is doubtful if any ever will'.

He had been a hero to boys all over the country.

Other players from the age who are in the all-time top twenty batsmen include Andy Sandham, Wilfred Rhodes and Tom Hayward, of whom Wisden noted in the 1914 edition *that 'in the course of the season of 1913…..had the satisfaction of rivalling WG Grace's feat of making a hundred three-figure scores'.*

But perhaps the most remarkable player of the period was the Yorkshire all-rounder George Hirst. In 1906 he performed the unique double of taking 208 wickets and scoring 2,385 runs. In one match he scored 111 and 117, and took 6-70 and 5-45. Not even Botham in his pomp could match that!

Pity poor Northamptonshire! After becoming a first class county in 1905, they were skittled out for just 12 against Gloucestershire in 1907 – still the lowest score in a first class match - and the following year for 15 against Yorkshire. In 1907, Charlie Blythe of Kent, who sadly was to be killed in France in 1917, took 17-48 against them – all in one day! All was not lost, however, as they surprisingly improved to finish second in the Count Championship of 1912 and fourth in 1913.

Given that cricket reflected the time, the popularity in the Golden Age of the Eton and Harrow match is not surprising. It was not played at either of the two schools, not even at one of the more picturesque grounds in adjoining counties, but at Lords, then as now the most prestigious and famous cricket ground in the world. It was important - back then, Eton vs Harrow mattered a lot — and not just for the public-schooled elite. It was representative of the 'public school code' - focussed not on academic achievement, but on sport – and the heart of this code was cricket, exemplifying the character of the Englishman. The code was aspirational to all schoolboys, encapsulating as it did the spirit of fair play, courtesy and adherence to authority and the rules.

Everyone supported one school or the other. So, not only was the ground packed - the match in 1914 was attended by over 38,000 people during its two days - but it was followed all over the country.

Folks would have been particularly enthralled by the 1910 fixture – 'Fowler's Match'. No need to go into detail; suffice to say that it was one of the greatest cricket matches of all time, rivalling the famous Headingly Test of 1981. Wisden declared that *'In the whole history of cricket, there has been nothing more sensational'* and The Times said that *'A more exciting match can hardly ever have been played'*.

Perhaps the best example of the blurring of the lines between being English, the public school code, and the values of cricket are exemplified in Sir Henry Newbolt's famous poem, Vitae Lampada, written in 1897, and which I'm sure would have been well known to the school pupils of Hambleden:

> *There's a breathless hush in the Close to-night --*
> *Ten to make and the match to win --*
> *A bumping pitch and a blinding light,*
> *An hour to play and the last man in.*
> *And it's not for the sake of a ribboned coat,*
> *Or the selfish hope of a season's fame,*
> *But his Captain's hand on his shoulder smote --*
> *'Play up! play up! and play the game!'*

> *The sand of the desert is sodden red, --*
> *Red with the wreck of a square that broke; --*
> *The Gatling's jammed and the Colonel dead,*
> *And the regiment blind with dust and smoke.*
> *The river of death has brimmed his banks,*
> *And England's far, and Honour a name,*
> *But the voice of a schoolboy rallies the ranks:*
> *'Play up! play up! and play the game!'*

> *This is the word that year by year,*
> *While in her place the School is set,*
> *Every one of her sons must hear,*
> *And none that hears it dare forget.*
> *This they all with a joyful mind*
> *Bear through life like a torch in flame,*
> *And falling fling to the host behind --*
> *'Play up! play up! and play the game!'*

The Olympic Games were held in London in 1908. The most famous incident of the games came at the end of the marathon. The first to enter the stadium, Dorando Pietri of Italy, collapsed several times and ran the wrong way. Not far from the finish line two of the officials went to his aid. Pietri eventually crossed the line in first place, but the runner-up, American Johnny Hayes protested, leading to Pietri's disqualification. Since he had not been responsible for his disqualification, Queen Alexandra awarded him a gilded silver cup the next day. The rowing events were held in Henley from 28 - 31 July, which must have been a huge attraction for the men and women of Hambleden.

The period gave rise to several national heroes for children all over the country to look up to, one of which, Robert Baden Powell had already made a name for himself during the siege of Mafeking before he formed the Scouts and later the Girl Guides. We know there was a scout hut in Hambleden behind the Village Hall (in what is now the garden of Hamblebrook House) - though we do not know when this was erected. Scouts were an important organisation for boys before the War - indeed, the original constitution of the Hall dating from 1962 states that a representative of the Scouts has an ex officio seat its management committee.

The Hambleden Parish Magazine of June 1914 names the Scoutmaster as Mr Heath (the school headmaster), and extols the virtues of scouting:

> 'the aim of the Association is to develop good citizenship among boys by forming their character, training them in habits of observation, obedience and self-reliance, inculcating loyalty and thoughtfulness for others, and teaching them services useful to the public and handicrafts useful to themselves. The object of the movement is to make them like those fine, brave, loyal men and women who have opened up new countries, such as the backwoods of America, and the veldt of South Africa.'

The Parish magazines of the years leading up to the outbreak of war include several sketches of boys in scout uniform, representing the Christian ideal of what all boys should aim for. In the Bucks Free

Press of October 1917, comment was made of two local men who had been awarded medals for bravery in the field (Lance Corporal Joseph Tilbury and Private William Bond) that they were *'up to the time of their enlistment, members of the local troupe of Boy Scouts, who are very proud of their fellows' splendid conduct'*.

Florence Nightingale died in 1910. Her fame began in the Crimean War and she had used these experiences to found modern nursing. She was well known as a prodigious and versatile writer; many of her books on nursing were written in simple English so they could easily be understood by those with poor literary skills.

Rudyard Kipling had made his name in the Boer War and became one of the most popular writers in England, in both prose and verse, in the late 19th and early 20th centuries. Many of his books and poems have become standard texts, and Our Men would have been introduced to them at the village school. Typical are these lines from his 'Children's Song', written in 1906:

> *Land of our birth, we pledge to thee*
> *Our love and toil in the years to be,*
> *When we are grown and take our place*
> *As men and women with our race.*
>
> *Teach us to rule ourselves alway,*
> *Controlled and cleanly night and day,*
> *That we may bring, if need arise,*
> *No maimed or worthless sacrifice.*
>
> *Land of our birth, our faith, our pride,*
> *For whose dear sake our fathers died;*
> *O Motherland, we pledge to thee*
> *Head, heart and hand through the years to be.*

Although nowadays these lines seem rather jingoistic, Kipling had merely voiced sentiments that were universally held to be part of the national heritage. Patriotism was the watchword, and nobody was questioning anything. His books in their day were seminal works – novels such as 'Jungle Book', 'Just So Stories', 'Kim'; many short stories, including 'The Man Who Would Be King'; and poems, including 'Mandalay', 'Gunga Din', 'The White Man's Burden', and 'If'. In 1907, he was awarded the Nobel Prize for Literature, making him the first English-language writer to receive the prize, and to date he remains its youngest recipient at 42.

The exploits of explorers such as Shackleton and Scott would have thrilled Our Men. They would have grieved at the death of Scott and his comrades, with the honourable way in which Captain Oates sacrificed himself for his comrades being regarded as the essence of the values of the day. Shackleton, in fact, set sail on his historic voyage to Antarctica just four days after war was declared in 1914.

The great magician and illusionist and a major celebrity of the day was Harry Houdini. Houdini visited Britain on several occasions, making his first visit in 1900 when he appeared at the Alhambra Theatre in London; further tours took him all around Britain visiting major cities including Glasgow, Liverpool, Birmingham, Leeds, Manchester and Bristol. People flocked in their thousands to see his shows and to experience his many outdoor appearances where, shackled in handcuffs and chains, he would regularly leap from bridges.

In 1904, the Daily Mirror challenged him to escape from special handcuffs that it claimed had taken Nathaniel Hart, a locksmith from Birmingham, five years to make. Houdini's performance at London's Hippodrome Theatre was reported to have been watched by 4,000 people and more than 100 journalists.

Another celebrity who would have been held in awe by Our Men was William "Buffalo Bill" Cody, the famed American soldier, bison hunter and showman. He had toured with his Wild West Show since 1882. The show began with a parade on horseback that included US and other military, American Indians, and performers from all over the world in their best attire. Turks, Gauchos, Arabs, Mongols and Georgians, displayed their distinctive horses and colourful costumes. Visitors would see feats of skill, staged races, and sideshows. Many historical western figures participated in the show - for example, Sitting Bull appeared with a band of twenty of his braves.

Cody's headline performers were well known in their own right - people such as Annie Oakley and her husband Frank Butler did sharp shooting. Performers re-enacted the riding of the Pony Express, Indian attacks on wagon trains, and stagecoach robberies. The finale was typically a portrayal of an Indian attack on a settler's cabin. Cody would ride in with an entourage of cowboys to defend the settler and his family.

The Wild West Show toured Europe eight times. It was enormously successful, making Buffalo Bill an international celebrity and an American icon. In all he visited over 270 towns in Britain, including both High Wycombe and Reading, where it might not be to fanciful to think that some folks from Hambleden might have been in the audience. His last tour of Britain was in 1904. Although his fame spawned many other showmen bringing their own vision of the American West to the fairgrounds of Britain, it was the personality and charisma of Buffalo Bill himself, which fascinated and thrilled the audience, and even those, as in Hambleden, who would have only followed his exploits through the columns of magazines and newspapers.

But perhaps the hero that would have the greatest impact on the lives of Our Men was Herbert Kitchener. Kitchener became a national hero in 1898 for winning the Battle of Omdurman and securing control of the Sudan, after which he was given the title Lord Kitchener of Khartoum. In the Boer War he played a key role in the conquest of the Boer Republics; his responsibility for the detention of Boer women and children in what became known as concentration camps tended to be overlooked.

Ever since Khartoum, the country had felt an almost religious faith in Kitchener; a sort of mystic union seemed to exist between him and the British public. His remoteness from Britain undoubtedly helped to nurture the Kitchener legend. The initials 'K of K' were a magic formula, and his broad martial moustache a national symbol. His weaknesses – intolerance of interference and opposition, inability to delegate responsibility, the disregard of normal procedures, and acting as his own chief of staff and military secretary – were unknown to the public, and overlooked by his political masters.

In 1914, at the start of the Great War, he became Secretary of

State for War and a Cabinet Minister, though he found it difficult to adapt to the concept of collective responsibility. Lloyd George wrote that *'his main idea being to tell the politicians as little as possible, and to get back to the War Office as quickly as he could decently escape'*. His imposing visage became the chief recruiting poster - the moustache, the eyes and the enormous pointing finger were to bore into the soul of every young man between the ages of 19 and 30. From shop windows, at railway stations, on the sides of buses and trams, and in schools and town halls, Kitchener's iconic face was soon glaring out accusingly: he wanted YOU for the army. For Britain to have gone to war without Kitchener would have been as unthinkable as Sunday without church, and there would have been public uproar. He embodied so much of Britain – he was the most famous soldier in the world.

Our Men benefited from the 1870 Education Act which made school attendance compulsory for children up the age of 13 (it would rise to 14 in 1918). Although education was basic, they were well versed in the three R's, and having a fair degree of literacy, were no doubt keen to read the information and entertainment that only newspapers could supply - they were the internet of the day. Rather like the recent dot-com boom, between 1866 and 1914, 4,000 newspaper companies were formed in London and the provinces. The Bucks Free Press began publication in 1856, The Henley Advertiser in 1868, and The Henley and South Oxfordshire Standard in 1892.

Of huge influence on Our Men as youngsters would have been the weekly Boys Own Paper; each year's issues were bound together and sold as the Boy's Own Annual. Often published were adventure stories, notes on how to practice nature study, sports and games; puzzles, and essay competitions. One of the stories in the opening issue was 'My First Football Match', and the first volume's serials included 'From Powder Monkey to Admiral, or The Stirring Days of the British Navy'. In the same volume, Captain Matthew Webb contributed an account of how he swam the English Channel.

The paper unselfconsciously promoted the British Empire as the highest achievement of civilization, and reflected fully the racist attitudes which were taken for granted in Britain at the time.

One of the most popular national titles was a magazine called Tit-Bits (or to give it its full title, *Tit-Bits from all the interesting Books, Periodicals, and Newspapers of the World*). Normal sales were about 500,000, though when it ran competitions with cash prizes, circulation could shoot up to 2,500,000. The emphasis was on human-interest stories concentrating on drama and sensation. Short stories and full-length fiction were also incorporated, including works by authors such as Rider Haggard and P. G. Wodehouse.

The leading newspaper publisher of the day was Alfred Harmsworth (later Lord Northcliffe). He realised that the schools were turning out hundreds of thousands of boys and girls who were anxious to read and who did not care for ordinary newspapers; they had no interest in society, but would read anything that was simple and sufficiently interesting. He started out publishing comics and journals for children – Comic Cuts, Illustrated Chips, Boys Home Journal, Marvel and Boy's Friend were among his titles.

Northcliffe was an early pioneer of tabloid journalism. In 1896, he began publishing the Daily Mail in London - which was a glittering success – modestly priced, simply written, noisy, conservative, scaremongering, sporty, full of human interest and medical quackery, larded with competitions, and stridently imperial in tone: *'We know that the advance of the Union Jack means protection for weaker races, justice for the oppressed, liberty for the down-trodden'* declared an editorial in 1900. It was the perfect product for the new age of wider literacy brought about by Victorian educational reforms, and by the time war broke out was selling nearly a million copies a day.

Taglines of The Daily Mail included "the busy man's daily journal" and "the penny newspaper for one halfpenny". Prime Minister Robert Cecil, Lord Salisbury, said it was "written by office boys for office boys". However, WH Smith did not let his closeness to Salisbury stop him from making a fortune from the distribution of the Mail and other Northcliffe titles, which included the Sunday Dispatch, then the highest circulation Sunday newspaper in Britain, the Daily Mirror, the Observer, The Times and The Sunday Times.

Northcliffe's publishing portfolio meant that he controlled four out of every ten morning newspapers, and his editorials wielded great sway over all sections of society.

The Boer War had enabled Northcliffe to establish, beyond popular doubt, his reputation as the spokesman for patriotic Britain. His views were reflected in his editorship of the Daily Mail in the run-up to the Great War, when the paper displayed a virulent anti-German sentiment and was thoroughly in favour of sending millions of young men to fight on the continent. This led rival newspaper The Star to declare, *'Next to the Kaiser, Lord Northcliffe has done more than any living man to bring about the war'*.

Our Men would have been hugely influenced by them and no doubt they would have been one of the main reasons they were prepared to abandon their homes and go to war. The WH Smith family had made their fortune by riding on the back of this publishing boom, and I think we can be confident that they would have made sure that newspapers were available in Hambleden in the period leading up to the War – the building that is now the Sports and Social Club was the Reading Room.

Our Men had been brought up in interesting times; not only interesting, but also peaceful. True, there had been wars, but they had been far off colonial ones, like the Zulu and Boer Wars in South Africa, on the periphery of Europe like the Crimean War (the details of which may have been familiar to the folk of Hambleden as Lord Cardigan, he of the Light Brigade, had been born in the Manor in 1797), or short and decisive like the Franco-Prussian War and the Russo-Japanese War. And now all these were over, and the major European powers could enjoy the tranquillity of peace and all that it offered. In fact planning had started in Britain for the centenary of the Battle of Waterloo, in which the fact that for a hundred years no British army had shed blood in Western Europe was to be celebrated. Besides, the rapidly globalising world of the last pre-war years was meshed together by trade and communications – there was no incentive to fight each other.

The century had started with the Paris Exposition of 1900. This bold exercise in cultural diplomacy showed that the scars of the Franco-Prussian War of 1870 had ever so slowly begun to heal, and the Exposition's general atmosphere of cheeriness filled everyone with a sense of security and optimism that Europe would enjoy peace and prosperity for years to come. It was a perfect symbol of contemporary pride in material and moral progress, a gathering *'destined'* – as the Berlin chamber of commerce wrote to its Parisian counterpart – *'to bring the civilised nations of the world nearer to one another in the labours common to them all'*. Why would Europe want to throw it all away? And so rapidly – thirty-seven days after Archduke Franz Ferdinand and his wife Sophie Chotek arrived at Sarajevo railway station on Sunday 28 June 1914, Europe was at war.

The truth is that this golden age of security belied an atmosphere of increasing international tension and uneasiness. The crises that punctuated the years after 1905 would erode the peace – crises over Morocco, and crises, above all, in the volatile Balkans, where the newly independent state of Serbia exercised a powerful attraction on Slavs living within the Austro-Hungarian Empire, and where Austrian and Russian interests clashed head-on. Meanwhile in Germany, Tirpitz was building up the navy while Britain looked nervously on.

One of the most popular sub-genres of late Victorian and Edwardian literature was the invasion fantasy – the most famous examples of which are Erskine Childers's The Riddle of the Sands and HG Wells's The War of the Worlds. Such authors profited from the growing unease with Germany by publishing scare stories in which Germany, real or imagined, replaced the traditional enemy, France. Their books were not only bestsellers, but in a cycle that seems quite common in the history of intelligence, the books themselves contributed to a certain perception of Germany. The period before the Great War was a great time in Britain for spy stories - in the last years before the war German spies seemed to be everywhere, and were a standard topic in the columns of the Daily Mail, the Daily Express and similar newspapers. Even the greatest detective of all times came out of retirement to stop the Germans. In 'His Last Bow', a short story published in 1917, Arthur Canon Doyle described how Sherlock Holmes broke up a vast and very efficient German spy ring just as the war was beginning.

The outbreak of the war was accompanied by an outburst of British paranoia over German espionage, and the police had to investigate hundreds, even thousands, of denunciations. Such denunciations failed to produce any genuine spies, though in early

August, twenty-two spies were arrested on the advice of the fledgling MI5, which, at this time, consisted of only 17 staff (including the caretaker); one of these spies was executed by firing squad at the Tower of London in November. Ten more spies were to be executed during the course of the War - shot by firing squad either in the old miniature rifle range in The Tower of London or The Tower's ditch. Spy fever then turned into an attack on enemy aliens, with calls in the Daily Mirror and John Bull for all Germans to be interned. The authorities did little to stop the fever; indeed, they used it to pass the Defence of the Realm Act at the beginning of August 1914 that gave the government wide-ranging authoritarian social control powers during the war period. The exhibition halls at Olympia were requisitioned to serve as what the Home Secretary rather insensitively called 'concentration camps' for enemy aliens – this after the public furore over the treatment of Boer women and children towards the end of the Boer War only a few years earlier. The captives were held in roped-off enclosures under the big dome (except for a minority who paid for the privilege of being housed in the restaurant). Five lavatories served 1,200 men. Alexandra Palace and a workhouse in Islington were used as London's other internment centres

If, with the benefit of hindsight, we now know that fears of a German invasion in 1914 were groundless, it must not be forgotten that many, including Kitchener, viewed it as a very real possibility at the time, especially after the bombardment of Scarborough and Hartlepool in December 1914.

Wars are made by individuals, and one hundred years on the characters still seem familiar: at their apex were the grandest Europeans of all – the continent's monarchs whose qualities and defects defined the countries of which they were the head: the United Kingdom's George V, dependable and dull; Wilhelm II of Germany, erratic and proud; Nicholas II of Russia, loyal and conservative to some, easily led and weak to others. Together these three – all cousins of one another, all descended from Queen Victoria, George and Nicholas so alike in looks that they could be mistaken for each other – personified the European family of nations. When all three gathered in Berlin in 1913 for a royal wedding, it seemed that no harm could befall the world so long as Europe's dynasties remained so intertwined – a testament to the underlying goodwill between the nations. Who could have foreseen that within the next five years one was to be murdered (Nicholas), one would be forced into exile (Wilhelm), and the third would change his family name (from Saxe-Coburg-Gotha to Windsor) to secure his dynasty. It was Europe's tragedy that none of these men, nor most of the chief politicians and military men that served under them, possessed the imagination to foresee what was to come, and to stand out against the pressures building up for war.

While there is broad agreement about the consequences of the War, the causes have always been contentious. In many ways, it has a damning simplicity: the Germans started the war in order to win; the Allies fought so as not to lose. Britain, in the aftermath of the costly and embarrassing South African War, feared Germany's desire for a place in the sun, especially the Kaiser's naval arms race which he believed would lead his nation to greatness while threatening Britain's empire. France's decision-makers exhibited a fierce pride to regain their nation's former glory and to exact revenge for its humiliating defeat at the hands of Germany during the Franco-Prussian War of 1870-1871. Russia, the behemoth of Europe, with close ties to other Slavic nations in the Balkans, especially the Serbians – who unwisely flaunted their growing independence in the face of the decrepit, yet still dangerous, Austrian-Hungarian Empire – played a critical role in the lead up to war. Germany, with its unstable Kaiser Wilhelm II, the oddest of all the intermingled and inbred royalty of Europe, both wanted war and feared its consequences. New treaties and old grievances, when combined with hard-liner ultimatums and dangerous complacency, all set Europe on the march to war.

Naval rivalry was the crux of Anglo-German antagonism. Grand-Admiral Tirpitz believed that Germany was engaged in a life-or-death struggle for its rightful place among the community of nations, a struggle that could only be won with a powerful fleet. Germany had intended the naval race to be a means of forcing Britain to be friendly, but instead persuaded her to not only to seek to outbuild Germany, but to abandon her preferred aloofness from Europe and draw closer to Russia and France, forming an Entente Cordial. The Entente Cordiale was a calculated defensive measure, but the fact is that alliances conceived as defensive by those who make them can easily appear offensive to others. Consequently, Germany formed a Triple Alliance of the Central Powers – Austria-Hungary and Italy (though eventually Italy fought with the allies in the War, having decided that the allies were more likely to indulge her ambitions for colonial aggrandisement).

We have to remember that countries and alliances are made up of people, and it was decisions made by a score or so of men (and they were all men) in half a dozen capitals that led to war. And it was the human weaknesses of pride, honour, vanity and the competitive drive for imperial conquest - how much a country was willing to endure in terms of taking a blow to its sense of pride and international standing - that drove Europe to war. In particular, it was the Kaiser who, after the murder of Archduke Franz Ferdinand, gave his ally, Austria-Hungary, carte blanche to exact vengeance on Serbia, which had spawned the assassins – the so called 'blank cheque'. He could not bring himself to take the one decision – withdrawing his support from Austria-Hungary – that would have prevented Russia and then France from entering the conflict. And he authorised the violation of Belgian neutrality, without which Britain might have not have fought at all.

The nations of Europe could have pulled back from the brink, but failed to do so for fear of looking weak. A certain sense of honour prevented any retreat. As the Russian prime minister summed up, *'We do not want a war, but do not fear it'*. They should have done. Science and technology, which had brought so many benefits in the nineteenth century, also brought new and more dreadful weapons. After the lessons of recent battles such as Omdurman, where British rifles and machine-guns had slaughtered the massed ranks of Dervishes, and Colenso, where Boer Mausers and machine guns had mown down massed ranks of Britons, we can only wonder how the top brass on both sides failed to learn that modern warfare was mechanised and brutal.

Simply because only a very few anticipated the Armageddon to be unleashed, Europe walked over a cliff into a catastrophic conflict which would kill millions of its men, bleed its economies dry, shake empires and societies to pieces, and fatally undermine

Europe's dominance of the world. British wartime Prime Minister David Lloyd George later wrote, *'The nations slithered over the brink into the boiling cauldron of war without any trace of apprehension or dismay.'* Historian Christopher Clark refers to them as 'sleepwalkers' – *'watchful but unseeing, haunted by dreams, yet blind to the reality of the horror they were about to bring into the world.'*

Did Britain have a choice? Many supporters of intervention in 1914 argued that Britain had led France to expect its help, and that it would be dishonourable to back out. Moreover, for Britain to have abandoned France and Belgium to their fates would likely have left most of Europe under German control; domination of Europe by a single power had been a nightmare that the British had fought and schemed against for over 300 years. Once the Germans held both France and Belgium, they would have controlled the Channel ports from Ostend and Zeebrugge to Brest, which could have been used as bases for the German navy to threaten the British fleet and empire. The conclusion that can perhaps be drawn is that unless so many young men had not risked their lives, a militaristic Germany would likely have built a European superpower. As Foreign Secretary Sir Edward Grey told the House of Commons on the eve of the declaration of war:

> *'I do not believe for a moment that, at the end of this war, even if we stand aside, we should be able to undo what had happened…to prevent the whole of the west of Europe falling under the domination of a single power….and we should, I believe, sacrifice our respect and good name and reputation before the world and should not escape the most serious and grave consequences.'*

However, the historian, Niall Ferguson in his controversial book 'The Pity of War' argues that the escalation of the War to global proportions was entirely Britain's fault. According to Ferguson, Britain's entry into the War transformed a continental conflict into a world war, which was then badly mishandled, necessitating American involvement. His case is that Britain should have let Germany defeat France, and then turn to Russia. The War was not inevitable, Ferguson argues, but rather the result of the mistaken decisions of individuals. And yet, as Ferguson writes, while the War itself was a disastrous folly, the great majority of men who fought it did so with enthusiasm.

The War had huge geopolitical consequences that rumble on to this day. In the aftermath of the War the victors at the 1919 Peace Conference at Versailles sought to punish Germany and its allies, while remaking the modern world in ways that affect us still. The peace settlement, while thwarting German ambition and causing the dissolution of its empire, was a significant cause of the economic and political turmoil that made possible the rise of Hitler and the Nazis; in Russia the War contributed to a revolution that led to seven decades of totalitarian rule, and later the Cold War. Whereas the War saw the emergence of Japan and the United States of America as significant powers of the twentieth century, it finished the Ottoman Empire, and transformed Turkey from an Islamic sultanate to a constitutionally secular republic, but one which carried a burning resentment against its Greek neighbour for lifetimes to come. The Austro-Hungarian Empire was no more. It was broken up to create the new states of Czechoslovakia, Hungary and Austria. The state of Yugoslavia was conjured out of the morass of the Balkans - but left a legacy that would rumble on for the next hundred years. It consigned the great aristocratic dynasties of the time, the Romanovs, the Habsburgs and the Hohenzollerns, to history, and so weakened the colonial powers that ended on the winning side, Britain and France, that they became dependent on America for their own security. The ensuing peace treaty laid the seeds of conflict in the Middle East by its wholly arbitrary creation of Iraq, Syria, Lebanon, Transjordan, Palestine and eventually, of Israel. In short, it has shaped the world since 1918 – it was the seminal event of modern times.

Hambleden

These homes, this valley spread below me here,
The rooks, the tilted stacks, the beasts in pen,
Have been the heartfelt things, past speaking dear
To unknown generations of dead men,

Who, century after century, held these farms,
And, looking out to watch the changing sky,
Heard, as we hear, the rumours and alarms
Of war at hand and danger pressing nigh.

From 'August, 1914' by John Masefield

It was General Stanley McChrystal, Commander of U.S. Forces Afghanistan in 2009 who said that 'Wars are ultimately determined in the minds of populations'. In the Great War, the home front mattered almost as much as the battlefront. Persuading people to sustain the war effort meant satisfying their belief that the war was worth fighting. The purpose of this chapter is to try to examine some of the elements that may have gone into the peculiar chemistry that formed the individual mind-sets of the people who lived in Hambleden in 1914. What was the village like that Our Men left? How did they live, how did they work, how did they enjoy themselves? What formed their characters, so that they were prepared to accept the deaths of so many of their young men.

Until August 1914, a sensible law-abiding Briton could pass through life and hardly notice the existence of the state beyond the post office and the policeman – who at the turn of the century in Hambleden was one PC Crook! He could live where he liked and how he liked. He had no official number or identity card. He could travel abroad or leave his country forever without a passport or any sort of official permission. Rather like us, he could exchange his money for any other currency without restriction or limit, and could buy goods from any country in the world on the same terms as he bought goods at home. He would not recognise the multi-cultural, diverse, European world of modern Britain. Nor would he recognise the constant involvement of British forces in combat somewhere in the world. In every year since 1914, British forces have been engaged in conflict; in 1914, apart from a few colonial conflicts and a thirty-month campaign in Crimea, Britain had been at peace for 100 years. Consequently, unlike the countries of the European continent, the state did not require its citizens to perform military service. A Briton could enlist, if he chose, in the regular army (like Our Man Percy Clinkard), the navy (like my grandfather) or the territorials (like Our Man Brian Molloy). He could also ignore, if he chose, the demands of national defence – there was no need to worry as he had every confidence that the greatest navy in the world would ensure that his island was safe.

It is true that things were changing. A reforming Liberal government was elected in 1906. Provision was made for old age pensions to be paid - hardly generous at only five shillings a week, a paltry sum even in those days, and only paid to people over 70. Nevertheless, it was a start. Although the economy was stable in the years 1900-1914 and unemployment was fairly low, the first labour exchanges in which jobs were advertised were set up, and in 1911 the government passed an act establishing sickness benefits for workers.

However, in an agricultural community like Hambleden, in which livelihoods depended on landowners, many of these regulations were seen to be irrelevant. What did affect life in Hambleden, though, was the introduction of measures aimed to improve the quality of rural life. The Agricultural Holdings Act, passed in 1906, allowed farmers to farm their holdings without interference from landlords. Further legislation sought to limit the degree to which fixtures and improvements remained the property of landlords, and sought to increase the number of small farmers.

The position of landowners was further undermined by the famous 'People's Budget' of 1909 - the first budget in British history with the expressed intent of redistributing wealth. A 'super tax' was introduced on incomes over £5,000 (£450,000 today), and more controversially, the Budget included a proposal for the introduction of a complete land valuation and a 20% tax on increases in value when land changed hands. Of all people, it was Winston Churchill who justified this attack on the landed classes as follows:

> *Roads are made, streets are made, railway services are improved, electric light turns night into day, electric trams glide swiftly to and fro, water is brought from reservoirs a hundred miles off in the mountains – and all the while the landlord sits still… To not one of these improvements does the land monopolist as a land monopolist contribute, and yet by every one of them the value of his land is sensibly enhanced.*

The traditional pattern of life might have been under threat, but in Hambleden the evidence is that it was still ordered by the estate owners, owners of large houses and the Church. We might not notice the stirring of these social tectonic plates if we stepped out of our Tardis at the village pump, under the shade of the two large chestnut trees, in early 1914, for the infrastructure of the village centre would look very much as it does today…....apart from the War Memorial (obviously!), the trees themselves and the pump, which would, of course, be working – in fact, we might even see a queue of people waiting to use it. Not that we would be able to understand them! The local accent then was a lot broader than today – the village was pronounced 'Hammulden'.

The village is described wonderfully by Charles Gray in his book 'Born on Chiltern Slopes' - the village of his childhood in the 1920's would not have been very different from that of ten years earlier, and is even not so different today. Although many properties have changed use from commercial to residential over the century, and many have been extended, it would all be very familiar.

The stream would be there, though I doubt it was more than a trickle in March 1914 as the total rainfall for the previous twelve

38

months was   only twenty three and a half inches; we know that annual rainfall must be at least thirty inches before the stream runs. It would certainly not be the torrent it is today in March 2014. The state of the stream was a regular feature in Parish Magazines of the time – for example in July 1903 it reports that despite rainfall of six inches in June (against an average for the month of two inches) the brook *'has not yet come back to life'*, although there are *'rumours of activity in the springs of Colstrope'*. Whereas the stream is to us merely an attractive feature of our village, in 1914 it would have been vital to the watering of livestock. If it ran dry, animals would have to be driven to dewponds or water pumped from wells would have to be taken in carts to the fields.

We would notice more people in the village going about their business – women shopping at Johnny Ponds' shop, men at the blacksmith (David Williams) and the harness maker (Edward Harris), folks at the Post Office. We would also notice a number of folks on bicycles, and maybe even the odd car. We would see many animals – a herd of cows being driven through to a fresh pasture, a few people on horses, some pulling carts, clip clopping along. There were more horses than people in the village in 1914; for every Land Rover and tractor we see today, there would have been two or three horses. Did anyone clean up after them, I wonder? Many horses, of course, would be requisitioned by the army in the War.

We might have heard the sound of the traction engine in the wood yard, which was approximately, where the surgery is today. It was operated by John Hollier of Coombe Terrace. What we would not have heard is the whistling of our wonderful red kites. Few folks in Hambleden in 1914 would have recognised a red kite; in fact, they would probably have tried to kill the poor animal if they had seen one. We regard the kites as ubiquitous and take them for granted, but they had been driven to extinction in England by human persecution by the end of the nineteenth century. Gamekeepers had poisoned them to protect game bird chicks, as had farmers to protect young lambs; we now realise that they feed mainly on carrion, worms and insects. Kites would remain extinct in England until 1989 when birds from Spain were imported and released into the Chilterns. They started breeding in 1992 and now there are over 600 breeding pairs in the area.

If we got our timing right we would have seen the children pouring out of the school on the rise just behind the village. One hundred and sixty children attended in 1914, though it was rare, if ever, that the full complement was in attendance. In 1914 the headmaster was a Mr Heath, before him a Mr Willis; their daily Log gives us a fascinating insight into the day-to-day workings of the school. Boys were often kept away to work on the farm. Parents would withhold their children for inclement weather – for example 14 February 1900 *'due to snow, roads impassable; only 40 turned up for school, but were sent home. School closed for the week'*; 18 October 1903 *'weather very wet and stormy – attendance poor (138)'*.

Infectious diseases were a scourge – in May 1901 it was recorded that *'3 families have scarlet fever – the medical officer examined all children. No further cases were found, but several parents kept their children away'*. Later that month the school was closed by the Medical Officer of Health on account of the fever. Similarly in May 1903 an outbreak of diphtheria was noted. The Medical Officer of Health again inspected the school buildings, and again the school was closed until further notice. It reopened in early June, but five days later the Headmaster records *'low attendance (104) due to families infected with diphtheria and very wet weather'*.

School holidays were frequently granted – half days were granted when the regatta was on; even so *'attendance very poor in the mornings'*. On 31 May 1900 a half day was granted *'for rejoicing over the supposed entrance of Lord Roberts into Pretoria'*. June 1902 was almost a continual holiday – a half day was granted on the 2nd to celebrate declaration of peace; another half day on the 4th as a 'school treat'; a whole day on the 17th because of the choir and church workers outing; and finally on the 28th, a half holiday to celebrate the Coronation (of Edward VII).

Before we get the idea that schooling was a bed of roses, perhaps we should note that corporal punishment inflicted on both sexes was common. In February 1900 the Head records that he *'caned several boys for being in the girls' playground and for injury to school premises by snowballing.'* In 1901 the School Inspector noted *'The scholars are orderly, but the excessive frequency of corporal punishment argues serious defects in the moral training of the children.'*

One can sympathise with the Head. His log frequently refers to shortages of equipment, especially a lack of books. The School Inspectors' reports note *'The school must be kept properly supplied with books'; 'more reading matter is wanted. The present musical instrument is useless and should be replaced by a serviceable one'; 'the gallery in the infants classroom is an inconvenient structure – it would be a very good thing if dual desks - on the floor - were substituted.'*

Getting and keeping good staff was a constant problem – the inspectors' report of 1904 notes:

> *'The school is suffering, like many others, from a shortage of staff, but it is kept going considerably by Mr Willis. I wish that something could be done to improve the surface of the playground.*
>
> *Infants: The condition of the infants is not the strongest feature of the school, but here again the want of a complete staff is felt. I hope it will improve when it is taught under normal conditions. There are no desks other than those on the gallery, which are so packed together so as to make it impossible for a teacher to get near the occupants. The equipment in this respect is bad, and it should be entirely remodelled and renewed.'*

A former pupil remembers in the WI publication 'Buckinghamshire Within Living Memory'

> *'We first wrote in sand trays with our fingers in the infants' class, later with pencils, then dipping our pen nibs into inkwells in our desks.*
>
> *The boy and girls had separate playgrounds, with outside bucket lavatories.*
>
> *The District Nurse would examine our heads to see if we were clean!'*

Most of Our Men attended the school – two of them are commended several times in the Headmaster's Log - Ralph Tilbury and Alfred Dawson. Others are noted as either joining or leaving; Silvester Valentine joined on 13 March 1903, a month after his fourth birthday! It's not surprising infants were only allowed to write with their fingers in sand!

Having noted the school, it would not take us long to see that the villagers of Hambleden were, well, dirty! In France the battlegrounds were a sea of mud. Curiously some men were apt to say it was not as bad as home. Agricultural labourers had swopped one field of mud for another. At home, mud permeated daily life everywhere. A walk to the shops meant mud on the hem of a dress. Mud on unpaved streets squished over the stoutest boots, splattering everything. Servants would spend hours cleaning long skirts that had swished over streets where horse droppings steamed and gutters overflowed. Swilling the step into the house, the path to it, and a tiled or stone-flagged hallway was a daily task.

For those who worked on the land, mud was traipsed into the house. In many Hambleden houses the floor was hardened earth which could soften unpleasantly in prolonged rain – and then you had permanent indoor mud. The farmyard stank, the sweating workers stank; life on the land was no elegant picnic. There was no bucolic paradise in living cheek by jowl with poultry and pigs.

Rural life was desolate – a constant struggle to get food on the table. Although they were surrounded by good land and healthy livestock, the average family did not eat well, and could only just survive. Countrywomen were not carefree apple-cheeked lasses bearing baskets of apples to market; they were second-class citizens often leading very narrow lives and worked to the bone. They had large families, little income, and were called on to pick potatoes, make hay, feed the livestock and keep the family going. Women would not wash in the mornings, as there was nowhere private, as the men got ready for work. Added to which there was the range to riddle, the floor to swill, water to boil, candles to trim and oil lamps to fill. Boys may bath once a week; girls could go months without washing their hair.

Living conditions were basic and crowded. The population of the Parish in 1911 was very similar to what it is today (about 1,500), but houses today are larger, and there are more of them. We can scarcely conceive of the number of persons crammed into a few rooms in the early twentieth century. The 1911 census records the following: John

Garrett lived with his wife, three daughters (aged 16, 10 and 1), two sons (aged 13 and 9) and a lodger (8 bodies in all) in a 4 room cottage at Rotten Row; George Edwards lived in a 4 room cottage in Frieth with his wife, three daughters (27, 19, 2) and four sons (12, 10, 8, 5) - 9 bodies in total. The twelve year old was Our Man Arthur Edwards. Incidentally, Mrs Edwards had borne fifteen children in her 29 years of marriage; two had died. She was 50. Another nine-person Frieth family, the Clacks, also lived in four rooms. And there are many, many more such examples.

Not only were workers' cottages overcrowded, but also living conditions were poor. Piped water and electricity did not arrive until the 1930s; before that the oilman came round weekly to deliver paraffin and oil for lamps, candles, matches and other household goods. Water had to be pumped from a well. Bathrooms and inside lavatories were for the wealthy few; workmen would have had just a sink indoors and a long wait for water heated on the kitchen range. It was common practice for parents to share their bedroom with at least one child. Cottages were structurally unsound – rotting window frames, leaking roofs, earth or rough stone floors, always damp and cold in winter.

In the Parish Magazine of 1871, Canon Ridley had written about living conditions in the village:

> '…..there is abundant room for a yet further advance. There are houses which no amount of care and labour on the part of the occupiers can make even <u>decent</u> dwellings for a labourer and his family.'

In his study of rural working conditions in 1913, Benjamin Seebohm Rowntree noted:

> 'Their domestic water supply must be drawn laboriously, bucket by bucket, from wells, the purity of which is not above suspicion. Their thatched roofs, if they do not leak, become in winter half sodden sponges of rotting straw exhaling odours of mildew, while the slate slabbed floors, which are laid upon clammy clay, are always cold and darkened here and there

by patches of damp which show where water is lying. The treads of the stairs are worn into holes and warped to disclose crevasses with rat-gnawed edges. Ventilation they have in plenty, for no door or window is watertight, though the chinks in the casements and frames are stuffed with brown paper. Parts of the houses are in dungeon darkness because of the inadequacy of window spaces, the greenery that clads them on the outside and the pallid pot plants on the sills. There are corners of rooms that no natural light has ever illuminated'

Nice!

A member of the WI, remembered a slightly more rosy way of life in 'Buckinghamshire Within Living Memory':

We cooked on the old-fashioned range in the kitchen. There was no thermometer and my mother would open the oven door and quickly put her hand in to feel the heat. She could tell the right moment to put the food in. We had to heat the irons on top, one in use and one getting hot, and we had to be sure to clean the iron well before use. There was a built in copper in the corner of the scullery which had to be filled with water and a fire lighted underneath on washing day.

Lamps and candles gave light and open fires heated the rooms, with oil stoves in the bedrooms.

We got water from a well nearly 100ft deep. There were two 16 gal buckets, one up and one down. To operate it one turned a wheel sited on a platform nearby. The water was delicious, clear, sparkling and very cold even on the hottest day.

Many of the cottages had only rainwater that was collected from the roof into an underground tank. The housewife was quite adept at drawing water in a pail using either a rope or a pole to let the bucket down into the tank. Quite often the pail was lost in the tank and a neighbour with a pole with a hook on would help to retrieve it.

During hot weather, a bar was placed across the opening of the tank and a bucket on a rope attached to it. Meat and butter were placed in the bucket and it was hung down in the tank, which was always cool.

We had a tin bath that we used to stand in front of the kitchen fire and fill with water that came from our two rainwater butts. One night my mother got the rainwater in after dark, popped the lid on the boiler, and when it was piping hot and poured it into the bath, only to find we'd boiled up a frog and the poor thing had boiled white. We just couldn't face a bath that night.

When a bucket fell into the well there would be a shout 'Fetch the snitchers'. This was a four-clawed device on a rope which could hook up the bucket.

The lavatory at our cottage was about 60ft up the garden, and was a wooden seat and bucket variety, which had to be emptied into the Guzzle Hole – a big hole dug in the garden into which all waste matter was placed. Keeping the candle alight and running up the garden on a cold, windy or rainy evening was not very easy, especially when you are terrified of the dark.

My father employed an elderly man in the village to empty our lavatory bucket into a pit on the common. This, of course, would have been done during the hours of darkness. He once fell over with the bucket, and never did this job again. Who could blame him!

My grandmother steadfastly refused to buy toilet paper, considering it a sinful waste of money. Squares were cut from her weekly magazine, and were threaded at the corner with string. We were never short of reading material in our lavatory.

Many villagers used the contents of their lavatory bucket to enrich their gardens. It was considered particularly good to put in the celery trenches, and the finest celery was produced. I have never liked celery!

The parish boasted two industrial concerns – Barnett's flourmill at Mill End and the West and Collier chair factory at Frieth. Apart from these, a few clerical jobs and one or two chauffeurs, all men worked on the land – for one of the two estates, for tenant farmers, or as gardeners for private individuals. Unlike today, Hambleden men were largely dependent on individuals for their livelihood, and, more often than not, their housing. To that extent, it was still a feudal society, in which the landowners and the Rector were the arbiters of good behaviour.

Those who could afford to do so always hired domestic assistance. This is a feature in the world of 1914 which today we would find striking: the regular presence of non-kin as part of the household. In fact, this was the real and visible interface between the classes in 1914 – in the household, and to a very large extent between women. To understand the village that Our Men left, we need therefore to look at the folks to whom Our Men would have doffed their caps, or touched their forelock – the employers of servants, or servant keepers.

To discover more about these servant keepers we might wander along to the Stag and Huntsman and chat to the Landord, Frank Sherlock, who was a rather venerable 63 in 1914. He was not to know that his eldest son, Henry, would die of wounds in Mesopotamia (roughly modern Iraq) in November 1917, and would be buried in a war cemetery in Baghdad. (I wonder if the cemetery is still there?) His name is on our War Memorial.

In 1914, there were two major estates in Hambleden. The oldest established estate, which included the Manor House, was owned by Major Frank Scott Murray (the Squire), who had inherited it from his father, Charles, in 1909. The Scott Murrays had lived in Danesfield until 1887, in which year they moved back to Hambleden - although the family had purchased the estate in 1802, they had leased the House out. It was Charles that planted the glade of giant Wellingtonia trees on the hill opposite the Manor, so that he could extract the last drop of sunlight from the setting sun – you can still see the glade today if you walk along the path through the woods above Woolleys. In the 1911 census the Manor is listed as having 30 rooms, and having eight live-in servants.

The estate under the Scott Murrays bore the brunt of the crippling agricultural depression as grain prices collapsed under the flood of cheap imports from the New World after 1875. Free trade meant that British farmers could not respond. Markets for stock and dairy products and perishable cash and fruit crops also suffered from foreign competition with the development of refrigeration and canning after

1870. A rare positive was the growth of dairying with produce sent to Oxford, Reading, London and the Midlands by railway. The estate suffered and became run down – it is likely that the Scott Murrays were asset rich, but cash poor. Several local men emigrated to seek a better life. Our Men, the Gray brothers emigrated to Canada in 1912, subsequently to fight and die with the Canadian forces in the War; in May 1903 the Parish Magazine published a letter from New Zealand *'It is 29 years since we left Hambleden......'*. The same journal noted in October 1914 that Gilbert Silvester (a carpenter, the older brother of Our Man, Valentine Silvester. The family lived on Dairy Lane, and worked at Greenlands), has just started to seek his fortune in New Zealand (where he joined the Canterbury Mounted Rifles).

The situation was not helped by the 'People's Budget' of 1909, increasing taxes on landowners; eventually Frank Scott Murray would sell the Manor and the estate to Frederick Danvers Smith, 2nd Viscount Hambleden, in 1922. Some 85 years later the estate, comprising 44 houses and cottages, the pub, village stores and 1,600 acres, but not the Manor House, was sold to Urs Schwarzenbach, a Swiss financier.

In April 1907, there would have been much excitement in Hambleden when Frank Scott Murray married Miss Jane de Trafford. The journal 'The Tablet' gives us a fascinating insight into a society wedding of the age:

> *The marriage between Miss Jane Seymour de Trafford, daughter of the late Mr. Augustus de Trafford, of Haselour Hall, Tamworth, and Mr. Francis Scott-Murray, late Oxfordshire Light Infantry, eldest son of Mr. Charles Scott-Murray, of Manor House, Hambleden, Bucks, was solemnised at the Brompton Oratory, on Thursday in last week. The ceremony was performed by the Bishop of Birmingham, assisted by the Rev. John O'Toole, in the presence of a large number of friends and relatives. The bride was given away by her brother, Mr. Henry de Trafford. She wore a beautiful diamond pendant, the gift of her mother. There were six bridesmaids and two train-bearers in attendance. The bridesmaids each carried a crook, on which were pink roses and lilies of the*

valley, and wore diamond and turquoise heart brooches, the gifts of the bridegroom. Mr. Austin Scott Murray, brother of the bridegroom, acted as best man. Before the Nuptial Mass, which was celebrated by the Rev. J. Pereira, of the Oratory, Birmingham, the Bishop of Birmingham gave a short address on the dignity and sanctity of Christian marriage, and then read a telegram from the Holy Father giving the Apostolic Blessing to the bride and bridegroom and wishing them a long life and happiness. After the ceremony a reception was held at 38, Grosvenor Gardens, kindly lent for the occasion by Lady Lovat. Later in the day the happy couple left London for the Riviera, where the honeymoon is being spent.

Several people from Hambleden were among those that gave a wedding present:

Mr. and Mrs. Holt Beever, coffee service; Mr. and Mrs. JL Molloy, clock; Major and Mrs. Luard, links; Mr. M Molloy, links; the Hon. FWD and Lady E Smith, pearl and diamond pin; Mr. EC Grenfell, bridge table; Employees of Hambleden estate, silver bowl.

In June, the Parish Magazine reported that *'the village was gay with flags in honour of the celebration of Mr Frank Scott-Murray's marriage with Miss J de Trafford, which took place shortly after Easter. The Squire and Mrs Scott-Murray entertained the work people on the estate and others of their neighbours in the Couchfield Meadow.'*

The other major family in Hambleden was, of course, the Smiths at Greenlands. Much has already been written about the family, and its history is well known. William Henry Smith (son of the founder of the eponymous company) bought Greenlands in 1868, having made a fortune from selling books and newspapers at railway stations. To ensure adequate heating and lighting, he built a gas works across the Henley Road; the 1911 census shows Harry Hare of Greenlands as being a 'gas stoker'. So that he could keep in touch with Whitehall and Head Office, he installed a private telegraph office. Although he further extended the building, its appearance received a cool reception from Jerome K. Jerome who joked in Three Men in a Boat (1889) that it was *'the rather uninteresting-looking river residence of my newsagent.'*

As the influence of the Scott Murrays declined so that of the Smiths increased. This was part of a general trend throughout England, as the influx of middle class families into rural areas ('new' money) disturbed the old order of squire, parson, farmer and labourer. It was a gradual change as the rural working class no longer came to accept uncritically the traditional structures, and the urban world was coming more and more to define the views and aspirations of rural people. It was the era of Victorian and Edwardian altruistic paternalist industrialists who sought to create a better life for their employees – George Cadbury, William Lever and the Bolsover Colliery Company come to mind. While the Smith involvement was never on the scale of these, the motivation was similar.

Many people in the village depended on the Smiths for their livelihood and housing. The 1911 census lists 62 people - servants, estate workers, wives and children - living in Greenlands or a Greenlands property. This number excludes those who worked on the estate but who lived elsewhere, and is artificially low as Viscountess Hambleden was not in residence at the time, so her personal retinue of twelve servants would have been with her in her prestigious London home at 23 Belgrave Square (now the German Embassy).

The Smiths were great benefactors of the village. As well as developing the Greenlands estate, William Henry's son, William Frederick Danvers Smith, 2nd Viscount Hambleden (known as Freddie, who inherited the title on the death of his mother in 1913), built the museum, the school, the headmaster's house, the dispensary and associated accommodation and the Working Men's Institute and Reading Room. As well as these very visible improvements to our village, their less obvious support of local organisations was much appreciated. In 1914 alone they kept the local district nurse (Nurse Pullen) going by a donation to her costs of £30 (about £3,000 today) as well as picking up the costs of improvements to the Parish Room, including a new floor in the small room, and internal decoration of the caretaker's house (some things don't change!) The Parish Magazine commented that *'fortunately we learn that Lord Hambleden intends to do this, so we have much to thank him for...again.'*

He was particularly concerned with the frequent outbreaks of diphtheria, typhoid and scarlet fever; Sally Strutt in her interesting book 'A History of the Culden Faw Estate' tells us that as well as improving the housing, health and education of the Parish, WH Smith left money in his will towards the Smith Isolation Hospital on the Fair Mile in Henley which included a Hambleden ward.

They made a donation of £4 to the Hambleden Rifle Club for ammunition and rifles - the shooting range was in the field behind Bacres Farm. Local men had a reputation for being good shots – in 1906, Our Man Ralph Tilbury of the Church Lads' Brigade received a prize at the Rottingdean Camp for being the best shot at the Camp shooting competition.

The Smiths were keen supporters of the churches in the Parish, in 1914 donating £15/8/0 to Hambleden Church and £3 to Skirmett Church (which was always struggling for money). Freddie Hambleden was much exercised by the plight of the Church in Wales. In March 1914 the Parish Magazine *'regretted that there were not more on February 23 to hear Viscount Hambleden and Mr Maddocks of Cardiff explain what is proposed for the four Welsh dioceses in the current bill before Parliament.'* (Why were they surprised?!)

The Magazine further reported that leaflets were distributed supporting the Church in Wales. It commented that if Hambleden was treated as it is proposed to treat the Church in Wales......

'......there would be nothing left for the maintenance of the clergy of this parish : except the Rectory and the profits of the Dean, which is not strictly speaking the part of the Glebe from which the cricket ground is taken, but the other part including 'the island'. This with two little strips, on either side of 'Parsonage Hill' was added to the glebe by Sir Matthew White Ridley, when the patronage first came into the Ridley family : all the rest of the Church property of the parish was given before 1662 and would therefore be confiscated. Tithe payers

*should note that they would still have to pay tithes, though
they would not go towards the maintenance of religion.'*

I'm glad that's clear!

Standing at the pump and looking up the hill above the Parish Room (as it then was called) we would see the imposing fifteen room Rectory, now Kenricks, in which lived the Rector, AH (Herbert) Stanton, his wife Edith, daughters Mary, Hilda and Rose, and three servants. Edith Stanton was the sister of Mrs Cripps of Parmoor (later to become Lady Parmoor), and of Beatrice Webb, the economist, socialist and social reformer, who coined the term 'collective bargaining'. Along with her husband Sidney Webb and numerous others, Beatrice co-founded the London School of Economics and Political Science and played a crucial role in the forming of the Fabian Society. Her views must have had some influence on the Stanton family, which may seem an apparent contradiction to the traditional view of a rural parson of the age, and would suggest that perhaps the Hambleden of 1914 was not quite as feudal as we might suppose.

Herbert Stanton had become the Rector in 1896, and would stay in office until 1936. In 1927 he wrote the wonderful history of Hambleden 'On Chiltern Slopes', which is a must for anyone interested in the story of our village.

He was a wise and kindly man, as we have noted elsewhere when he commented on the outbreak of War. Perhaps the affection in which he was held in the village can be best illustrated by this charming description of the wedding of his daughter, Mary, on 23 July 1914, less than two weeks before the declaration of war, when the Parish magazine noted that *'nearly a thousand must have joined in the festivities'*. It is interesting to compare it with the report of the Scott Murray wedding noted above. I know which one I would rather have attended!

*'The day will be long remembered in Hambleden when the
first wedding after 40 years interval took place from the
Rectory. It was marked as a great day, and a half-holiday was
accorded to work-people. The bride walked up the aisle on the*

arm of her uncle, Lord Parmoor. Hearty cheers were given by the schoolchildren as the married couple went away in Lord Hambleden's carriage. Afterwards the children danced on the lawn of the Rectory: charming old country dances in costume, and the sword dance by the older children, delightfully accompanied by the piano and violin. These were followed by a Maypole round which younger children danced; the boys in smocks and coloured handkerchiefs, and the girls in white frocks and blue sashes. After the children, the older people danced until darkness came and rain, then with a long cheer for the bride and bridegroom and their parents and the singing of God save the King, we parted'.

In anticipation of the wedding, the following advertisement appeared in the June edition of the Parish Magazine:

'Miss Mary Stanton will be wanting early in September, for a flat in London, a Maid (single handed), any age over 25. Apply Hambleden Rectory.'

The parishioners presented the couple with a silver tray and candlesticks, the Hambleden Operatic Society presented a toast rack. Little did they know how their lives were about to change.
If we wandered into the churchyard, past the church, and looked to our left we would have seen Woolleys then, as now, an impressive country house. The 1911 census records it as having fourteen rooms, including the kitchen, but excluding bathrooms. It had three live in-servants – a cook, a housemaid and a footman.
The Molloy family moved from Kensington to Woolleys in 1882. The family consisted of James and his heavily pregnant wife, Florence, together with two sons, Brian and Maurice, aged six and five. Someone must have got their dates wrong, as daughter Clarissa was born on the day her parents took up residence at the house, her father dashing five miles to Henley for the services of a doctor. She was baptised in a private chapel in Danesfield. The chapel has since been demolished, but its stained glass and altarpiece are preserved in the Catholic Church of Henley.

The family were to live in the house for the next 34 years, during which time they would witness from their own front room the funeral of WH Smith in the Pheasants' Hill cemetery in 1891 and the building of the red brick villas opposite in 1912 by Mr Cook, the butcher, for his son and daughter.

The funeral of WH Smith was a big event in Hambleden. Although only a few of Our Men would have been old enough to remember it, it is worth repeating how it was described in, of all papers, the Huddersfield Daily Chronicle. Smith had died at Walmer Castle near Deal in Kent, his home as Lord Warden of the Cinque Ports, and his body was transported by rail (the paper goes into enormous detail on the various railway lines that were taken!), finally arriving at Henley.....

> At Henley Station the coffin was placed in a hearse with stained glass panels, and amid demonstrations of respect conveyed to Hambleden, where the interment subsequently took place. As the cortege proceeded along the route, about 100 carriages representing the principal gentry in the neighbourhood joined the procession, which was nearly half a mile in extent, and blinds were drawn at private residences, and in Henley business was partly suspended, the bells of the two local churches tolling in the meantime. Arrived at the lichgate of St Mary's Churchyard, Hambleden, some four miles distant, the corpse was met by the officiating clergy, the Rev. North Pinder (Rural Dean) and the Rev. C M Wetherell (rector of the parish), and the surpliced choir from St Paul's Church, Knightsbridge, who led the way into the sacred edifice, where the first portion of the solemn service was gone through. Afterwards a rather long journey had to be accomplished to the cemetery, which presented a dismal aspect after heavy rain. The service was concluded, the coffin being lowered during a heavy shower; and tears were shed by many of the large number of onlookers present during the singing of the hymn 'Now the labourer's task is o'er'.

Back to Woolleys - the head of the family, James Molloy, was an interesting man. Born in Ireland, he was called to the English bar in 1863, though he never practiced as a barrister. He was in Paris in 1870/71 and acted as war correspondent for one of the London dailies during the Franco-Prussian War. After the war, he developed a reputation as an accomplished French scholar and author; when he died, much later, his obituary recorded that he had written *'a delightful account of a rowing trip in France entitled 'Our Autumn Holiday on French Rivers' which ran into several editions and is still a reference book to the Seine and the Loire.'*

On returning to London for a time, he acted as secretary to Sir John Holker, attorney-general, and in 1889 was appointed private chamberlain to Pope Leo XIII, an honorary position.

But more than the above, he was best known as a musician. The Globe newspaper commented that

> *'Considering the universal popularity of his songs, which have been sung wherever our language is spoken, it is not going too far to describe James Molloy as a famous composer. We would venture to say that there is not a single British home able to boast a piano and singer that a few years ago did not know 'Love's Old Sweet Song'.*

James died at Woolleys in 1909, age 72, of pernicious anaemia. He left an estate valued at £2,030 (worth some £205,000 today), which doesn't seem that much in the scheme of things – but I suspect much of their lifestyle was financed by his wife, Florence.

Florence's father was Henry Baskerville, one time High Sheriff of Oxfordshire, and self-styled Lord of the Manor of Shiplake. He owned the famous 160-acre Crowsley Park estate, near Sonning Common, which since the Second World War, has been the site of a signals-receiving station used by BBC.

Stories about the family and its association with fierce dogs were among the inspirations for Conan Doyle's The Hound of the Baskervilles in which 'Sir Henry Baskerville' is a leading character. The book was published in 1902 and became a best seller, and it is perhaps not too fanciful to think that Conan Doyle was a houseguest at Woolleys. In any case, we can imagine Hambleden folk being intrigued with the links to one of their own neighbours.

One of the striking things to a contemporary eye about the middle classes in the pre-war years is the amount of leisure they enjoyed. Just as the employed working class appear to have worked terrifyingly long hours by modern standards, professional and commercial men, let alone upper and middle class women, seemed to have had a remarkably relaxed existence. One of the reasons we know more about how they lived was simply that they had more time than the workers to write letters and keep diaries. Such was daughter Clarissa, who had a flair for letter writing and it is thanks to her that something remains on record of the family's activities in the closing decades of the century. Corresponding with her niece Mary, she recalls the leisurely life led at Hambleden, much of it taken up by shooting parties, tennis, at which her parents excelled – the tennis court can still be seen from the fields and woods at the rear of the house - and sculling on the river.

Maurice was the youngest son. We don't know much about him, apart from the fact he was a good cricketer, representing Oxfordshire and Buckinghamshire between 1900 and 1905. He represented the MCC twice in matches at Lords. He died in Henley in 1965.

Their eldest child was Brian whose story is told elsewhere in these pages. He was the first Hambleden man to perish in the War; his name is on our War Memorial, along with that of the family gardener, Our Man Albert Willsher who died in November 1916 at Beaumont-Hamel.

The family were well connected locally. We don't know whether they attended Freddy Danvers Smith's wedding in 1894, but we do know they were guests at the Scott Murray wedding in 1907. Interestingly, in the census of 1901 Maurice was listed as a guest at the Manor, so one can imagine the families were close, both being Catholic.

Florence died in 1912, her will invoking some lovely images of the home .... *"To my son Brian I leave the cabinet in the hall at Woolleys; the carved armchair; the black engravings; the John Baskerville blue china; the eight Molloy spoons; and the oil paintings on the top landing"*.

To her second son Maurice she left.... *"my china, glass, books, pictures, prints, wines, liquors, furniture and other household effects...."* Such personal items must have ranked high in her estimation; I suspect Maurice was her favourite.

To her daughter, Clarissa, she left *"...all my plate and linen; my motor car; and all the rest of my estate, property and effects for her sole and separate use...."* Clarissa was a vigorous and vivacious person whose inheritance of her mother's motorcar - in a day when cars were few and far between - no doubt qualified her to take up ambulance driving, as she did in the War.

In 1916, Clarissa sold Woolleys, the scene of so much fun and games, music and laughter, but also sorrow and mourning, to a Major Drake.

About half a mile further along the valley from Woolleys we would come across the hidden gem of Bacres, another large (twenty-three room) country house and the home in 1914 of Mrs Alethea Louisa Riversdale Grenfell, the widow of the late Mr Henry Riversdale Grenfell, (whose death occurred in September 1902, and who is buried in the Pheasants' Hill cemetery). He had been a very well-known banker, becoming Governor of the Bank of England in 1881. By 1914 Mrs Grenfell was 84, but had led an active life in the community. She had been responsible for needlework in the village and nursing the sick - she was one of the group that started the Bucks County Nursing Committee. She wrote seven books on dressmaking, the most widely read being possibly 'Dressmaking: A Technical Manual for Teachers' in 1892. She learned Braille and spent the latter years of her life transcribing books for the blind.

At the time of the 1911 census she was living in her London house in Charles Street, Mayfair with her ten servants. Only the butler and his family were left at Bacres to keep an eye on the house while she was away. She died in 1923 aged 93. Her son Edward became a successful banker in his own right, and was the Grenfell in the influential investment bank Morgan Grenfell, since 1990 part of Deutsche Bank.

Other servant keeping houses in Hambleden included Hatchmans (formerly Colestrope Cottage), the thirteen-room residence of Frederick Hunter, a gentleman of private means, his wife and four servants.

The Hyde, although substantial, was occupied only by a Mrs Haddock and her two servants – though it would be purchased after the War by Major George Howson MC, an engineer who had served on the Western Front in the Great War, and who suggested to the British Legion that disabled ex-Servicemen could make poppies to be sold to raise funds for the Legion. The first Poppy Day was held on November 11th 1921 - the rest, as they say, is history! A cottage in the grounds was the birthplace of Our Man Frederick Plumridge; he was killed in October 1917 at the Battle of Broodseinde, near Ypres, and is remembered on our War Memorial.

Little Colestope was equally large, thirteen rooms, the residence of thirty year old Dr Wilson - a native of Banffshire in Scotland, his wife, daughter and two servants. Charles Gray tells us that he was only called out when the district nurse felt it necessary. He held a surgery in Vine Street in Hambleden – to find out where that was you need to read Charles' book!

Hambleden Cottage was one of several houses in the village that was named on Ordnance Survey maps of the time – along with the Greenlands, the Manor House, Woolleys, the Rectory (Kenricks), Yewden and Bacres. It was the home of Richard Luard, a retired army major, although only forty-nine in 1914. He was a widower, sharing his house with his daughter and six servants, one of which was a governess and another was a 'between maid'. The house was very substantial, having sixteen rooms. Major Luard was quick to respond to Kitchener's call to arms, for in September 1914 the Parish Magazine recorded *'Major Luard has been busily occupied as embarkation officer at one of the sea ports'*. Incidentally, his handwriting was immaculate, surely the sign of someone ideally placed to manage the logistics of getting troops across the Channel.

The house was the former home of Admiral of the Fleet Sir Alfred Ryder, who died in 1888 and is buried in the Churchyard.

Josceyne Lechmere, an author of private means, lived next door at Varnells with his wife and cook/housekeeper. Varnells is listed as having eight rooms, which the present owner tells me is about the size it is today. Joscelyne was a Roman Catholic, contributing articles to various Catholic journals – 'Lonely Catholics' in the Catholic Herald of 1937 and 'A Sussex Charterhouse' in The Commonweal in 1931. He published one book 'Pretty Polly – the History of Her Career on the Turf' in 1907, which is still available through second hand bookshops to this day.

Harold Heath, the headmaster, lived in the lovely School House, which like the school itself and the adjacent cottages, were built in 1897 in the Ruskinian Gothic Revival style. He shared the house with his wife, four year old son, servant (aged 13!), and two sisters in law - a fellow schoolteacher and a bookkeeper - all in six rooms.

I'm told that William Holt Beever, the land agent for the Smiths, was not a popular man – after all it was he that had to carry out some unpleasant tasks on behalf of the estate. He was recognisable as he rode around the estate on his white horse. He lived at Yewden, which in 1911 comprised sixteen rooms, with his wife and six servants. Apparently he only attended church when the temperature inside was acceptable, though he was a regular contributor to Church funds, as well as to the Rifle Club and the Nursing Association. The school headmaster noted in December 1901 that he presented portraits of Queen Victoria and WH Smith to the school on behalf of the Smiths (I wonder what became of them). In May 1902 school prizes were distributed by Mrs Beever.

In 1905 Mrs Beever paid for new churchyard gates in memory of her cousin, Ella Constance Freeman. The Parish Magazine reported that *'the gates are, happily, generally open, but those who avail themselves of the churchyard paths should remember that the paths are public only as leading to the Church, not for thoroughfare.'*

Thirteen of Our Men were from Frieth, and two from Skirmett, so a review of the great and good of the Parish would be incomplete without mentioning the worthies from those villages.

Skirmett was very much the poor relation in the Parish in 1914. The Parish Magazine has several references to the need for funds to keep the school and the church going. The major house there was Poynatts, the substantial (seventeen-room) home of Alfred Heneage Cocks and his two servants. The Parish has had its fair share of colourful characters and footnotes in history; Alfred Heneage Cocks was one such, a meticulous scholar and naturalist, an expert bell-ringer, and famous in Hambleden for his excavation, in 1912, of the Roman villa uncovered at Yewden at the turn of the twentieth century. He lived at Poynatts with a menagerie of owls, cattle, otters, wild cats and a collection of stuffed bats. Apparently, he slept with an alarming device, which entailed the firing of a shotgun at any night-time intruder fool enough to open his bedroom door!

His assistant, William Howard and his family lived in Poynatts Lodge; he listed his occupation in the 1911 census as 'wild animal keeper'!

Cocks supervised the building of the Hambleden Museum, erected just outside the village by Freddie Smith in 1913 to house the finds from the Yewden dig. The museum was opened by the elderly Viscountess Hambleden just weeks before her death.

The world first learnt about the Roman site in March 1917, when Cocks presented the results of his excavations to the Society of Antiquaries of London. *'The ground'*, said Cocks, *'was positively littered with the bones of babies... most of them newly born, but an occasional one was rather older'*. There were ninety-seven of them, making this the largest known such cemetery in the Roman Empire. Clearly, something unusual happened at Yewden, and archaeologists are still puzzling over it today. The remains were transferred to the Buckinghamshire County Museum in the sixties, and the site is now a wheat field.

Frieth was dominated by two large interests – the chair factory and Parmoor House, the home of Charles Cripps, later to become Lord Parmoor. Parmoor was a vast estate, larger than either the Scott Murrays or the Smiths in Hambleden, comprising just under 4,000 acres and including farms at Shogmoor, Flint Hall and Luxters. The family were political liberals - their son, Stafford, would become a prominent political figure in the 1930s and 1940s; between 1947 and 1950 he was Chancellor of the Exchequer – but in 1914 he was famous in Frieth for donating footballs to the local team! The Parish Magazine of August 1911 congratulated him on his recent marriage, but bemoaned his departure *'as a great loss to the football club.'*

Parmoor House consisted of twenty-six rooms, in which the Cripps family were looked after by seven live-in servants. In cottages on the estate lived the land steward, Thomas Jess, the coachman, William Hobbs and the carpenter/handyman, George Brazier.

During the Second World War the house was occupied by the

exiled King Zog of Albania. It subsequently became a nunnery, and is now the headquarters of the Sue Ryder Prayer Fellowship.

Charles Cripps was a generous donor to local causes – the Hambleden Rifle Club, Skirmett Church and Frieth Church, which was kept solvent by his donation of £100 (£10,000 today!).

His brother in law, Herbert Stanton who compiled the Parish magazine, would often gently tease him with phrases such as *'Lord Parmoor gave a speech memorable for its brevity'*, and *'Lord Parmoor addressed the Missionary Festival in an all too brief a way'*.

Despite the outbreak of war, the flower show was held at Parmoor on 6 August. The Parish Magazine recorded that because of rain *'we missed the attractions of the cricket match and tea, but with wise words the Squire told us the reason for dispensing with the usual merry-making, and we felt he was right, for War had been declared the previous day by this country against Germany, and the thought, though imperfect, of the horror of War had sobered us.'*

The War would have a profound effect on Cripps' political views, as he considered the decision to go to war a disaster. He opposed conscription and sympathised with conscientious objectors, who he thought were subject to excessive punishment.

No mention of Frieth would be complete without a brief look at the other important employer, church furniture makers, West and Collier. Except for those who worked for Lord Parmoor, West and Collier employed practically all the villagers – about forty men in the workshops (including master craftsman Alfred Hussey in the carving shed) or on their farm, which Thomas Collier had bought from Charles Scott Murray of Hambleden in 1895. The only part of the production that was not done at the factory was the caning and rushing of the seats, this being done at home by the workers' wives and children.

The product range included folding chairs designed and patented by Archie Collier (very similar to those used for Church Teas at Hambleden every Sunday afternoon in summer), churchyard gates, altar rails, choir seats, and lichgates – the lichgate at Frieth is one of their products. Customers could view their product range in the firm's London showroom at 6, Henrietta Street, Covent Garden. I don't think our conversation with Mr Sherlock in the Stag would have been complete without a mention of Henley, especially if our visit was around regatta time. In 1914, although geographically in Bucks, administratively Hambleden was part of Henley, and many commercial transactions would have been conducted there. The Parish Magazine contained twenty three adverts from Henley businesses, including a supplier of 'Best American Lamp Oil'; a builder of 'carriages, capes, hoods and windscreens to order'; an 'umbrella hospital', a tobacconist who urged customers to 'try our noted shags' (next door, the same man also sold 'pure sweets, dainty & wholesome'), an ice merchant and W Lawrence of Bell St who was, curiously, a cycle maker and supplier of gramophones and records. The opening of the railway in 1857 coincided with the late Victorian building boom, improving a hitherto sleepy market town to reflect the prosperity of the age, introducing paving and lighting, places of worship, a library, workhouse, hospital, police station and a court. This period of intense building activity has left a very distinct mark on Henley and has provided the town with a number of prestigious buildings, such as the Imperial Hotel in Station Street, built in 1897. In the 1890s, the corporation improved the town centre by demolishing some of the buildings at the more narrow road junctions, and in the same decade more houses were built beyond the railway station to the west side of Reading Road.

A number of large detached or semi-detached, well-detailed, villas and large houses were built, for example in St Mark's Road and St. Andrew's Road, to cater for the influx of upper and middle class professionals that moved to the town. Friar Park was built in 1890. By Edwardian times, Henley was in its heyday as one of the most fashionable towns in England. Its shops catered for prosperous townsfolk - five watchmakers & jewellers, two glass and china dealers, four hairdressers, two tobacconists, a musical instrument dealer, a piano maker and two chemists, as well as the more traditional blacksmiths, ironmongers, saddlers and harness makers.

Hambleden folk would have watched these developments with some interest on their occasional trips into Henley on market day, when perhaps, one of Henley's fifty-one (!) pubs might have been visited. In particular, they could not fail to have been impressed by the new Town Hall, opened in 1901. It is an impressive building now; we can only imagine how it must have seemed then.

Every edition of the Hambleden Parish Magazine included the railway timetable from Henley to Paddington, and to Oxford via Reading. Sixteen trains a day ran to Paddington and sixteen to Oxford, the first to Paddington leaving at 7.08 and the last at 22.08. The quickest journey to London took under an hour. Henley was promoted as a haven for commuters and *'for the toiler in the metropolis, a refuge of peace and rest after the worries of business'*.

As now, the highlight of the year, of course, was the Henley Royal Regatta. It had started in 1829 with the Oxford and Cambridge Boat race; had received Royal patronage in 1851; and graduated to a three-day regatta in 1886. It became part of the English social season, a place to see and be seen, a place of beauty and fashion. The Regatta added to Henley's attractions and by the end of the century the town was notable for its many boathouses, rowing clubs and hotels; the town became a sort of inland resort. In 1895 over 34,000 people visited the Regatta over three days; the town and surrounding countryside were packed – the larger houses of Hambleden would be full of houseguests. Servants would be running up and down stairs, carriages would be polished and hampers would be prepared. In 1901, WH Grenfell of Bacres stirred up the Stewards when he proposed the motion *'This meeting…while fully prepared to promote the establishment of an international regatta upon a proper course and under suitable conditions, is of the opinion that Henley Regatta does not provide either a proper course or suitable conditions for international competitions'*. The motion was soundly defeated! He died the following year.

Such an attraction of the rich and famous, dandies and beauties, must have been an irresistible draw to Hambleden folk. The school acknowledged as much by granting half day holidays during the Regatta – though the headmaster noted that attendances were still poor in the mornings! I expect boys and youths could earn a few pennies by rowing visitors across the river, and acting as general fetchers and carriers. Women would have been intrigued by the fashions. Exposure to society at the Regatta, and in fact exposure to Henley in general, surely made Hambleden folk realise that there was a world outside their village, and made it not such a rural backwater as perhaps we might believe. The Parish Magazines of the time support this view – folks were far from ignorant of goings on in the world – several references are made to outings, for example in July 1903

> *'....the annual outing to Weymouth of the Hambleden Church Choir .... by special excursion train from Henley. Among the various things seen was a sight of HM Convict Prison at Portland with the numerous convicts in their distinctive garb. The return journey was enlivened by dancing to the strains of a concertina and flute. Return to Hambleden was accomplished at 12.30 am'*

The school was closed twice in July 1900 for choir and church workers' outings to Earls Court, to ride on the Great Wheel and to visit the exhibition, and to Portsmouth.

Dependent for their livelihoods on personal service they might have been; country bumpkins they were not.

The event that would have involved Hambleden folks more would have been the Henley Show. In 1906 it was held at Mill End farm under the patronage of Charles Scott Murray, and in 1908 at Remenham Farm under the patronage of Freddy Smith. These events must have been such fun for the Hambleden folk – a real gathering of the clans. Men would have participated in the events - ploughing matches, rick building, thatching, shepherding, competitions for butter, poultry, eggs, vegetables, and, of course, livestock. No doubt, ale was consumed!

The Reading Mercury rather pompously recorded in 1892, on the occasion of the inaugural Show, that it hoped the event *'next Thursday will be as successful as it deserves to be. There is too little inducement in these days for farm labourers to become proficient in their work and any steps in this direction must be a considerable benefit'.*

Whereas the Regatta and the Henley Show were annual events, Our Men and their families had more regular entertainment in the village halls. Much more so than nowadays, the village halls were the social centres of the villages. The following are extracts from

Parish Magazines:
February 1914

> *The Yeomen of the Guard - 'Those who visited the Parish Room on January 12th and 13th could almost imagine themselves in the 16th century. On the rising of the curtain, we were faced with the 'Grim Old Tower' of London, most beautifully painted. More surprises awaited us. For there were yeomen in their red suits, Hambleden friends, but almost unrecognisable owing to their beards; Citizens in very gay clothes, and the women dressed in 16th century fashions.'*

March 1913

> *An entertainment was given in the Parish Rooms on 3 Feb in aid of the Parish Rooms Improvement Fund. After deduction of expenses, £3 0s 6d was handed over to pay the debt owed for improvement to the small room.*
> *Part 1 – A performance of 'Babes in the Wood'*
> *Part 2 – Songs and comic readings*

Regular games evenings were held (the equivalent, I imagine, of our Quiz Nights):
January 1905
Games evening, Hambleden v. Frieth. Everyone enjoyed the occasion of exchanging courtesies between the hill and the valley, but in the contest Frieth received 'a pretty bad beating'.

Sunday Schools:
February 1914

> *Sunday School – children performed old country dances, and the boys dressed up (in blue jerseys, white ducks and black shoes) for a spirited performance of the Sword Dance. During the interval four men sang songs etc and Miss Stanton played*

the violin. Afterwards two bran pies had been arranged. The dips afforded a good deal of amusement, especially when the ladies pulled out tobacco. The singing of Christmas carols and the National Anthem brought the evening to a close.

Talks on missionary activities:
January 1914

Frieth – on December 17, the village hall was crowded with an expectant audience to hear one of the clearest and most instructive addresses it has been my pleasure to listen to, on the non-Christian religions. The address was accurately illustrated with living pictures, and punctuated with prayer on behalf of the heathen, and native hymns.

April 1914

It was a real privilege to attend the Parish Room on March 18 to hear the Bishop of Yukon talk about the Church's work among the various races in his vast diocese – wild tribes such as Eskimos, Indians as well as Europeans. He spoke warmly of the hard-headed business Englishmen (the furtraders) who have dealings with these people.

The village halls then, as now, were always short of money:
January 1911

The Parish Room is now out of debt. £28 was paid for new doors, a gate a grate and the painting. Also this summer work will be carried out to draught-proof the windows and, we hope, to install a new stove.

February 1914

1. We have sold the piano that has for some time given so much trouble that it was thought best to part with it'. It was sold at auction for £7. With the profits of a Rummage Sale (£7 2s) we

*bought a strong second hand iron framed piano for £13/4/0
which it is hoped will keep in better tune and suffer less from
the damp and changeable atmosphere of the room.
2. A Curtain was provided for the new arch at a cost of £4/5/0.
3. After some 13 years' experience, the Trustees (Rector and
Churchwardens) have revised the tariff for the use of the Room.
Payment should be made when applying to use it.*

As today, from time to time folks would no doubt have felt the need for the odd pint. The Parish had several pubs – Charles Gray writes about them in his book. We've already mentioned the Stag, and the death of Mr Sherlock's son in the War. James Leaver of the Yew Tree in Frieth also lost his son, Frederick, who was killed in August 1917 near Ypres. His name is listed on the Menin Gate and also on our War Memorial. The landlord of the Royal Oak in Frieth, Edmund Barlow, lost his nephew William at Ancre Heights in 1916. William had lived at the pub.

A memory of how the pub fitted into life in the worker was left to us by Seddon Cripps, 2nd Baron Parmoor, and rather sums up the combination of paternalism, hard work, poor housing and relaxation that forged the characters of Our Men as they went off to war:

*Our carters....fed their horses about 5.00 a.m. and were in the
fields ready for work as soon as light came. They had their cold
tea and cheese or whatever they brought with them at about
8.30 a.m. and came back to the stable at about 11.00 o'clock
so as to escape the heat of the day. They then fed their horses
and went back to their own meal, returning to groom their
animals later on. Then they cleaned up their 'tack' and gave
their horses their evening meal, returning to their own high
tea, and going to bed early so as to be up at the right time the
next morning. There was then only candlelight in the cottages,
with an occasional lamp, so there was not much inducement
to read or write after dark, and they would often proceed to the
'local' at Frieth, or 'The Pheasants', where they could discuss
with their friends all parochial affairs.*

Happy days?

Our Men and the Army

The First World War, boys
It came and it went
The reason for fighting
I never did get
But I learned to accept it
Accept it with pride
For you don't count the dead
When God's on your side.

From "With God On Our Side" by Bob Dylan

The population of Britain, peacefully going about the daily business of unruffled life, paid little attention to reports of 'Trouble in the Balkans' which flared up so regularly that it seemed to be almost a fixture in the less prominent headlines of serious newspapers - rather in the same way we may tend, sadly, to skip over reports of another car bomb in the Middle East. To understand the reasons behind such incidents requires a far greater knowledge of history, geography and politics than the average reader possesses. So when Archduke Franz Ferdinand of Austria, heir presumptive to the Austro-Hungarian throne, and his wife, Sophie, Duchess of Hohenberg, were shot dead in Sarajevo, on 28 June 1914 by Gavrilo Princip, one of a group of six Bosnian Serb assassins, hardly anyone in Britain cared, or possibly even noticed.

It was evening before the news filtered through to the rest of Europe. Almost everywhere it had been a perfect summer's Sunday. The sun had shone; in Henley preparations were well under way for the regatta, and the Thames was bright with boating parties and rowdy groups of youths (some, no doubt from Hambleden) trying their skills as oarsmen between the marker flags. The day marked the anniversary of the coronation of Queen Victoria, an event still looked on with some nostalgia by many in Britain. The last thing people had on their minds was the possibility of a world war. Britain had not been involved in any major European conflict for many years. It had traditionally stood aloof from European quarrels and the tangle of enmities and alliances that maintained Europe's balance of power; and in any case, Britain was an island, defended by the most powerful navy in the world, the guarantor of freedom of the seas for the commerce that made Britain wealthy. Many believed that that if war was to come, the decisive battle would be fought not on land but at sea, when another Trafalgar would proclaim again that Britannia did indeed rule the waves. 'Jolly Jack Tar' was held in high esteem.

So how did Hambleden and the rest of Britain and the British Empire find itself at war only thirty-eight days later? No doubt it was a shock when war was declared, but it did not come out of the clear blue sky. Although clouds had been gathering over Europe for some time there was a feeling of confidence that statesmanship could deal with any threats and conflicts, build better and stronger international institutions to settle disputes peaceably, and make war obsolete. War with Germany may have been a spectre that had haunted Britain for the past decade, but over time its power of engendering fear had steadily diminished. *'A threat that goes on for too long ceases to have the effect of a threat'* noted HG Wells. If hostilities were going to break out anywhere, most people thought it would be at home where, by the summer of 1914, a civil war, a sex war and a class war seemed imminent or were already taking place. Ireland, the suffragettes, and the promise of a general strike by the trade unions created a background of widespread discontent.

It was only in the last week of July that most families in England began to have an inkling of the danger posed to them – what came to be known as the July crisis. Suddenly, they opened their newspapers to be confronted with the astonishing news of the threat of war, not from Ireland, but from the continent of Europe. On Friday 24 July Austria presented its demanding ultimatum to Serbia. Suddenly the

Ulster threat disappeared. As Churchill later poetically noted in 'The World Crisis 1916-18', *'The parishes of Fermanagh and Tyrone faded back into the mists and squalls of Ireland, and a strange light began immediately but by perceptible graduation to fall and grow upon the map of Europe'.* The historian, Mark Bostridge observed *'In the country at large, the developing crisis possessed something of the impact of a dormant volcano that had unexpectedly erupted.'*

What followed during the next week is difficult to follow by us even with the benefit of a hundred years of analysis; for those at the time it must have been mystifying. Could they have known how the Austrians coldly set out to destroy Serbia; how Berlin gave Vienna a 'blank cheque', assuring it of German support; how both countries ignored the certainty that Russia would pitch in on the side of its Slav protégé Serbia; how France would support its ally Russia; and how Germany's autocracy deliberately pushed Europe over the edge. How could they know that Germany recklessly gambled that Britain would stay out of the war, and that even if it did not, they felt sure they would win it within weeks by knocking out France, before turning to deal with Russia at leisure.

What became the tipping point for Britain was the issue of Belgium's neutrality. Germany's plan to outflank French troops involved a swift advance through Belgium – the so-called Schlieffen Plan. The British Government seized on a forgotten treaty of 1839 that guaranteed the maintenance and protection of Belgian territorial integrity in return for the country's neutrality. Up to the point that Germany invaded Belgium, the conditions in Europe were not sufficient to prompt British entry into the escalating European conflict. The majority in the Cabinet, under Lloyd George, were in favour of non-intervention; so for those that realised the necessity of war (including Prime Minister Asquith and Churchill) it became necessary to find something to persuade them. Belgium was the apparent *casus belli* – the 'weapons of mass destruction' - that politicians could manipulate to explain their rapid about-face on the subject, and that the public could seize upon as a just cause for war. Consequently, in response to the Belgian appeal for diplomatic intervention, Britain issued an ultimatum to the Germans demanding assurance of Belgian neutrality one last time. At midnight European time on 4 August, having received no reply, the British declared war on Germany. As David Stevenson eloquently states, '...*the British government went to war for reasons of calculated national interest, although it was able to unite opinion behind it because it appeared to be committed to an altruistic cause.*'

When Big Ben chimed 11pm on 4 August, crowds in Whitehall and the Mall linked arms and sang patriotic songs. In other parts of the country, and no doubt in Hambleden, the news was greeted variously - with shock, exhilaration, gloom and resignation. To many there may have been relief that the waiting was over, taking comfort that society was pulling together despite the industrial strife, suffragette militancy and Irish nationalism. Alternatively, perhaps folks were simply stupefied at the speed and finality with which Europe's long peace had ended, and accepted the coming of war with a sense of obligation, persuaded that their nation was the innocent party under attack from menacing foreign forces. Not everyone was as upbeat as a forty-year-old Churchill who wrote to his wife '*Everything tends towards catastrophe and collapse. I am interested, geared up and happy. Is it not horrible to be built like that?*'

The Rector, AH Stanton, wrote a very measured piece in the Parish magazine of September 1914:

> *Amidst the excitement of the war and our anxiety on behalf of those in whom we are specially interested, we must try not to forget the deeper aspects that should engage the attention of all thoughtful people; the terrible failure of our Civilization in Europe, that such a war should be possible : the sins, not so much of other nations, but of our own, that have brought upon us such a chastening under the hand of Almighty God.*

The same issue of the magazine published a most prescient letter written by the Bishop to all the parishes in his diocese:

> *Our thoughts, prayers and cares are all converted into one channel by the tremendous war. We are called to live through one of the great moments of history. A war of nations on so vast a scale, vaster than anything yet known in history,*

> *must in its issue involve tremendously deep social, as well as*
> *political changes, at home as well as abroad. It challenges us,*
> *therefore, as the Church of Christ in manifold ways. I believe*
> *we are nearly unanimous in feeling that our country could not*
> *have remained neutral : and no doubt, therefore, the primary*
> *challenge which the war makes to us is to be instant in prayer*
> *so that by our prayers we may effectively support our country,*
> *further the effects of the Allies on the terrible road to victory,*
> *and bring comfort to the wounded, the sick, the desolate, and*
> *peace to those fall in battle.*

The position of the Church of England must have been difficult – to reconcile the teachings of Jesus Christ with its position as the established Church, and as such committed to support the state's position in going to war.

Mind you, it seems that the clergy had its own little skirmishes to fight. The Parish Magazine of August 1914 noted that the Reverend Graham of Frieth *'fell off his bicycle and put his shoulder out in trying to circumvent a cow in the road'*! He recuperated with a holiday in Wales and Cornwall, and in September (with the Rector's 'generous permission'), he volunteered as a Chaplain to the forces.

It seems to me that Hambleden was particularly fortunate in having Herbert Stanton as its Rector, a man of some sensitivity. He might have had some sympathy with the following lines written in 1916 by JC Squire:

> *God heard the embattled nations sing and shout*
> *"Gott strafe England!" and "God save the King!"*
> *God this, God that, and God the other thing –*
> *"Good God!" said God, "I've got my work cut out."*

Having been aware of the likelihood of an European war for some years, and having been chastened by its experiences in South Africa some fourteen years earlier, when the power of the machine gun in the hands of defending forces was demonstrated over and over again, one would reasonably have thought that the Government might have prepared the army for what would lie ahead. Britain's defence policy at the time seemed to be one of 'decision by crisis'. Indeed, it is not clear that the term 'policy' was always appropriate in the pre-1914 context, given the looseness and ambiguity of many of the commitments involved. Fundamental decisions on defence matters, especially if they were likely to lead to higher expenditure, tended to be taken only when the international situation was sufficiently menacing to alarm the country as a whole, and when the government of the day therefore felt that the weight of public opinion was behind it. Until the Germans invaded Belgium and public opinion was mobilised in favour of a greatly expanded army, a wide gulf existed between Britain's military strategy and her actual military resources.

The army was singularly ill fitted for war: it was tiny, it was light on weapons (there were only two machine guns for every thousand-man battalion), it did not have conscription, and its higher command lacked the structures or expertise for European war - when war was declared there was not even a Secretary of State for War in the Cabinet. In being so inadequately prepared, Britain had pursued what Max Hastings calls a 'gesture' strategy, by which he means making a Continental commitment without an army designed for Continental war.

Why was the army so inadequate? The public's view of the army in the early twentieth century was, as now, slightly ambivalent. Not forcing men into uniform was a source of national pride. Despite a campaign for compulsory military service endorsed by the Daily Mail, the nation held a deeply held conviction that a volunteer, professional army was one of the things that distinguished Britain from its tyrannical neighbours. However, unlike the navy, the army was held in some suspicion. British soldiers had for centuries acted as a gendarmerie in the countries of the Empire before the establishment of a local civil police, and at home had 'aided the civil power' on many occasions putting down civil unrest. Indeed, as recently as 1911 two men had been shot dead by soldiers of the Worcestershire Regiment in Llanelli during demonstrations in support of a national railway strike, and in 1912, almost every available soldier was put on standby as London dock strikes threatened to turn into an uprising. This did nothing to enhance the popularity of the army, and made conscription politically impossible. It is not surprising, therefore, that the pre-war regular army consisted, on the whole, not of the cream of the nation, but of the hungry and homeless, the unemployable, those on the dodge from the law or from an irate father of an impregnated young woman, and young men rebelling against the authority of fathers or employers. In other words, for most, military life was a last refuge.......unlike today, when, in the aftermath of the conviction of Lee Rigby's killers, and with further cuts in funding, members of the army have rarely been so popular – unlike the conflicts to which they are committed.

By European standards in 1914 the army was small - contemptibly small, according to the Kaiser, though no evidence of his using this description has ever been found. It was probably a British propaganda invention, albeit one often repeated as fact.

At the start of the War Britain had a volunteer army of 247,000 regulars, 480,000 Reservists and Territorials, plus one or two miscellaneous units. The grand total was 733,000, of which 240,000 were in the Indian Army, stationed in India and other outposts of the Empire, and 269,000 Territorials who were not obliged to serve overseas. It was an army that was geared up for colonial warfare.

By contrast, Germany and Austria could call on 2.4 million troops in 1914, France 1.3 million and Russia 1.4 million. All of these were conscripts.

Clearly something had to be done! By luck when war was declared, Lord Kitchener, Britain's most famous soldier was still in England, on the point of returning to Egypt where he was British Agent and Consul-General. Asquith made a telephone call to Dover to halt his imminent departure, and asked him to return to London, where on 5 August, he was persuaded, reluctantly, to accept the post of Secretary of State for War. Kitchener's reluctance to get involved with politics is reflected in a comment he made to colleagues '*May God preserve me from the politicians*' and '*My colleagues tell military secrets to their wives, except Asquith, who tells them to other people's wives*'. Nonetheless his appointment was greeted in the country with universal relief –'*the tonic to public confidence was instantaneous and overwhelming*' said Asquith's daughter.

Kitchener, almost alone among his military and political colleagues believed that the war would be a protracted and costly business. He persuaded the Cabinet and the nation that Britain must prepare for a long war, and so on 6 August sought Parliamentary approval for increasing the size of the army to 500,000 men. The following day newspapers carried appeals for an addition of 100,000 men to join so called 'service battalions' of the regular army. Kitchener galvanised the young men of Britain to enlist by crossing through social barriers, and demonstrating that the army was no longer the last resort of the unskilled and the unemployed. Volunteers were to be between 18 and 30 years old, and were to sign on for three years or the duration of the war, thereby alerting the public to the possibility of a long struggle. These men were to be called the First New Army, or K1. By the end of the year a further four armies had been raised, bringing the total to 1,000,000 volunteers - the first mass army in British history. Later, in 1916, when the volunteer boom had fizzled out, the government was persuaded that it had no alternative but to introduce conscription.

We cannot know why Our Men joined up, or whether they were volunteers or conscripts. As conscription did not commence until early 1916, and given the time taken for training, we can perhaps assume that all those who died before December 1916 were volunteers (unless they were regulars or reservists). Fourteen of Our Men fall into this category:

Brian Molloy (a member of The Oxfordshire Yeomanry, a Territorial regiment)
Rowland Webster
Sidney Bond
William Collison
Alfred Dawson
Percy Clinkard (a regular soldier with the Gloucestershire Regiment)
Arthur Richardson
James Taylor
William Cook
George Gray
Harry Gray
George Hopper
William Barlow
Albert Willsher

Of course, the remaining Men may also have been volunteers –
we just do not know.

By the time Kitchener issued his first appeal, Britain was already
being swept by the sort of rising tide of patriotism that to modern
minds is difficult to comprehend. As well as the powerful pull of
moralistic patriotism and a well-defined sense of duty, the prospect
of adventure and the opportunity to escape from poverty, dreary
surroundings or a tedious job played their part in drawing men to
the recruiting offices. Indeed, the factors that impelled many to enlist
were as diverse as the recruits themselves. In small communities
such as Hambleden, I imagine the social and psychological pressures
on individuals must have been immense, especially after friends
and neighbours were seen to be joining up. Probably only a small
number had a single overriding motive for enlistment, most recruits
being driven to join by a combination of external pressures and
personal desires and loyalties.

A fair proportion of men who led the rush to the colours were
spurred on by a conviction that the war would last no more than a
few months and any delay in enlisting might rob them of the chance
to become personally involved in the greatest event of the epoch.

Like many myths about the Great War, we don't know whether
soldiers did indeed tell their families that they would be home
by Christmas; that the British public thought that the War would
be 'over by Christmas' is such a common feature of war fiction,
memoirs and histories that it has scarcely been questioned, let alone
seriously examined. What may have persuaded people to this view
was that in the Franco-Prussian War, the Germans had forced the
French to surrender in two months. They tended to overlook the
fact that it had taken the British three years to wear the Boers into
submission in South Africa, and that Kitchener was recruiting half a
million men.

Whatever the truth of the matter, the phrase has become
shorthand for naivety among a generation of young men who are
supposed to have rushed to join the army rather than missing all
the 'fun'. More realistically, and not unnaturally, we find predictions
of peace by various specific dates, and particularly by Christmas,

throughout the whole four years of the War as part of a coping strategy for both soldiers and civilians alike.

The prevailing opinion that the war would be short had precisely the opposite effect on some men – if it was going to be over so quickly, they saw no reason to abandon their domestic routine, especially if they had a family, and if, as with many in Hambleden, their house was dependent on their occupation. That initial enlistment returns of the first three or four weeks were disappointing may indicate that this was indeed the prevailing view; but once it became apparent that the war was going to be a long drawn-out affair, many felt it was their duty to sign up, and the bombardment of Scarborough, Hartlepool and Whitby by the German navy on 16 December 1914 was the final straw.

However, what caused recruiting to pick up in September was the news from Belgium. The destruction of Louvain struck a particular chord.

The city fell to the Germans on 19 August. It was relatively peaceful for six days until 25 August when shots were heard amid fearful cries that the Allies were launching a major attack. Once it became clear, however, that no such Allied attack was underway or even imminent, the city's German authorities determined to exact revenge upon Louvain's citizenry, whom they were convinced contrived the confusion that day.

The German form of retaliation was savage. For five consecutive days the city was burnt and looted. Over a thousand of the towns 9,000 houses were destroyed. Its library of ancient manuscripts was burnt, as was Louvain's university along with many other public buildings. The church of St. Pierre was similarly badly damaged by fire. The citizens of Louvain were subject to mass shootings, regardless of age or gender. By the end, some 250 out of a population of 10,000 were dead, including the mayor and the head of the university; many more had been beaten up. 1,500 inhabitants, from babies to grandmothers, were put on a train and sent to Germany where the crowds greeted them with taunts and insults.

As at other Belgian towns, the destruction of up to a fifth of Louvain's buildings merely exemplified a standard German strategy of intimidating the occupied Belgian people as a means of securing maximum civilian co-operation.

On 29 August photos of the sacking of Louvain were published in the press. Inevitably some of the more lurid reports of German atrocities were either wholly manufactured or grossly exaggerated; but still more had their veracity tested in the course of the war and were confirmed to be completely authentic. The British public did not have a mind to distinguish one from the other. Tales of 'murder, lust and pillage' contributed to the defining image of the enemy as the 'Hun'. Atrocity stories assisted recruitment by reinforcing the idea of war as a moral crusade. They also raised dark fears that England might face a similar fate should it be overrun by German invaders, and so the war became a defence of Britain. Rudyard Kipling encouraged men to sign up in his 1914 poem 'For All we have and Are':

> For all we have and are,
> For all our children's fate,
> Stand up and take the war,
> The Hun is at the gate!

From late August, Belgian refugees began to arrive in Britain, fleeing the German forces, bringing with them more horrifying tales of German bloodlust. This was the greatest flood of immigration since the arrival of the Huguenots at the end of the seventeenth century - 200,000 arrived in two months. The influx was widely covered in the press, and brought home to the British the full horrors and miseries of the war; the plight of the Belgians ('poor little Belgium') was used in propaganda posters that played a key role in persuading men to sign up. They showed examples of alleged German atrocities in France and Belgium; one such featured a contemplative British infantryman standing in front of Belgian refugees and a burning village. Such posters were intended to inspire enlistment through a sense of general anger about the plight of the Belgians, and to evoke enlistment through fear of what might happen should Britain be invaded.

Belgian refugees were housed in Henley. Their presence was commented on in the Parish magazine in October 1914:

> *The Harvest Thanksgiving took place on September 13, but we could not be unmindful of those harvest fields and gardens, not many miles away, devastated by war, and of the homeless and destitute of the Belgians and the French.*
>
> *The Belgian refugees who have come to Henley and neighbourhood will be somewhat surprised to see a destroyed church in this apparently peaceful land.*

(St. Mary's Church, Wargrave was completely gutted by a fire on 1 June 1914, thought to have been started by suffragettes).

In the issue of the following month, it was reported that

> *Lady Hambleden is most grateful to all her kind friends at Hambleden and Skirmett for their most generous help to her in making garments for the troops both in hospitals and at the front; also for their generosity on 'Pound day' in aid of Belgian Refugees at the Convent, Henley. The 'Pound Day' was most successful, and quantities of grocery, potatoes, flour etc were sent , also more than £50 in money.*

Lady Hambleden was later to translate a book expressing Belgian gratitude for the support they had had from Britain. Its introduction noted that:

> *In ten years, in a hundred years and yet longer, when the leaves of this book have turned yellow with age, nothing that it expresses will be forgotten. From generation to generation, the child sitting on his grandsire's knee will listen to the stories of the Great War and all its horrors. The tale of what England did for the poor exiles in her compassion and fraternal affection will ever move all hearts with a true emotion, and the story of the British campaign waged on behalf of suffering humanity will be rendered immortal by Belgian gratitude.*

At the same time as reports of atrocities in Belgium were filtering through to Britain, the British Expeditionary Force was experiencing difficult times. The British Expeditionary Force (BEF) had begun to cross to France on 7 August, only three days after war was declared, and by late August was engaged in a bloody and costly battle at Mons, with the retreat after the battle raising the spectre of another German walkover in France, as in the Franco-Prussian war of 1870-71. In fact, Mons was to be Germany's last relatively easy victory. Reports in the Times on 25 August noted that things had *'gone ill for the allies'*, and on 30 August, it published the influential 'Amiens Dispatch'. It described the retreat of the British from Mons on 23 August, and spoke of the *'terrible defeat'* sustained there; it described *'the broken bits of many regiments'* and British soldiers *'battered with marching'*. This article challenged the illusion of a short victorious war, and pointed out the vulnerability of the British army. It stressed that, although the BEF had *'won indeed imperishable glory, it now needs men, men, and yet more men'*.

This shocked the British public out of the notion of a short war and a decisive victory, and galvanised a recruiting boom, suggesting that men joined knowing that the war was dangerous. Indeed many joined precisely because there seemed to be a threat to their home, district and country. In addition, the famous Kitchener poster was first used on 5 September; by the end of September, over 750,000 men had enlisted; by January 1915, a million. As Margaret Asquith was reported to have commented about Kitchener, *'a poor general, but a wonderful poster'*!

Recruitment from urban areas was more robust than that in rural locations. Autumn 1914's harvest was an especially rich and plentiful one - hay and cereals were being harvested as early as 1 August - and undoubtedly played a considerable part in slowing down rural recruiting.

Farmers persuaded their men that working on the farm was a patriotic act in itself, and as vital to the country's interests in wartime as going off to war. In any case, skilled farm men, such as carters, cowmen, and ploughmen, were protected from enlistment. A less skilled man could also be exempted if his employer could prove his value by dint of the amount of wages he was paid.

On the other hand, some landowners positively encouraged their men to join up. Lord Burnham at Beaconsfield offered £10 (nearly £1,000 now) to every worker on his estate that was prepared to join up. We are unable to ascertain the views of the two major Hambleden landowners. We can imagine that they may have called all their men together and advised them accordingly. Perhaps landowners were more prepared to let domestic servants go: Sidney Bond was a hall boy to a Mr Simmonds at Wormseley, Stokenchurch, Alfred Dawson was a gardener in Pyrford, Surrey and Albert Willsher was a gardener at Woolleys. However, we know that several of the Scott Murrays enlisted in various regiments, and Freddie Hambleden was mentioned in despatches as a Lt. Colonel in the Devon Yeomanry.

For a young man the heady atmosphere which enveloped them in the early days of the war could easily prove irresistible, particularly if the army promised to provide the chance of escaping from an arduous, monotonous or depressing job that was devoid of prospects – and many jobs in Hambleden in 1914 were surely humdrum and promised nothing. Moreover, agricultural wages in Buckinghamshire were among the lowest in the country - about seventeen shillings a week for a 58 hour, 6½ day week, which could be a lot lower after deductions for payment in kind, or if the man was unable to work because of illness or bad weather. Compared with this, the army's eight shillings a week all found seemed quite attractive' especially if he was married and could claim nine shillings a week to be paid to his wife as a separation allowance (more if there were children).

The prospect of securing a permanent job with a reasonable wage was so poor that a number of Our Men had emigrated, and were in colonial regiments when they met their deaths – George Cutler, Harry Silvester and the Gray brothers, George and Harry, were in the Canadian forces; William Smith was in the 1st Btn of the Australian Imperial Force.

Whatever his motives and expectations, the mere fact that a man had resolved to volunteer did not, of course, guarantee that he would be taken by the army. He had to be between 18 and 30, be able to answer a few questions and pass a medical examination. The minimum height requirement was 5ft 6in (1.67 metres) and minimum chest measurement was 35½ inches (902 mm). Because of the poverty in which many potential recruits had lived, army doctors noted that malnourishment was so rife among applicants that 44%

were rejected as they were unable to achieve the minimum chest size. One may imagine that the life style of Hambleden men ensured they were in the other 56%! These entry requirements were amended from time to time to take into account whether the army had enough men or not. In any case, the standards of medical examination varied widely according to time, place and circumstance. In early Autumn 1914 when thousands were pouring into recruiting offices daily, it was difficult for doctors to perform anything but the most cursory examinations. One doctor was known to have examined 400 men a day over a ten-day period.

Indifferent, flippant, earnest, but all bored,
The doctors sit in the glare of electric light
Watching the endless stream of naked white
Bodies of men for whom their hasty award
Means life or death maybe, or the living death
Of mangled limbs, blind eyes, or a darkened brain;
And the chairman, as his monocle falls again,
Pronounces each doom with easy indifferent breath.
From 'The Conscript' by Wilfred Gibson

We know of two particularly tragic cases of men (boys) managing to avoid the entry requirements. The first is Our Man Alfred Coker of Chapel House, Skirmett who was killed on 3 September 1918, just two months before the end of the War, and just a month after his eighteenth birthday. Given that training took at least six months, he must have signed up under age.

The other is Our Man Arthur Edwards of Frieth, one of the fifteen children of farm labourer George and wife Emma. In 1911, seven of the children (age range two to twenty-seven) were living at home with their parents (nine bodies in all) in four rooms! Arthur was the eldest boy still at home; sadly, he was to die of wounds on 8 August 1918, aged nineteen. The Parish Magazine for September 1918 records '*There is not many an English lad who has spent the years of his life from his 15th birthday as he did - fighting for his country with one brief spell of respite*'.

Six others were killed while still in their teens and may well have signed up while under age - Ernest Batchelor, William Coker, Frederick Janes, Charles Leaver, Valentine Sylvester and Harry Vivian, who while still under age, went to France to work as a civilian behind the lines. He later joined up, and was killed on 19 October 1918 aged nineteen, little more than a fortnight before the Armistice – the last of Our Men to be killed in action.

Patriotic fervour was not limited to the young – the following must have signed up over age: Thomas Gearing (died age 38), Ernest Lyford (age 39), Brian Molloy (age 38), William Smith (age 42), Rowland Webster (age 47) and Sidney White (age 36). We know that Molloy and Webster were reservists in yeomanry regiments.

Having passed the entry requirements, a volunteer could choose for himself the unit in which he would like to serve. Naturally, most men opted to serve with their friends in a battalion of their local county regiment, although a few did prefer to go elsewhere. If the regiment of their choice was closed for recruiting, or if the volunteer was patently unfitted for that unit, the recruiting officer had the discretion to recommend an alternative. This would help to explain the spread of units of which Our Men were members.

The Bucks Remembers website lists 190 (yes, 190!) men from Hambleden, Frieth and Skirmett who fought in the Great War. As one may expect most (26) were in the Oxfordshire and Buckinghamshire Light Infantry of which 4 were killed; 12 in the Royal Berkshires (1 killed); 14 were in the artillery, and 6 in the Royal Flying Corps. Although the website only lists 2 men who joined the Royal Gloucesters, we have 5 men from that regiment on our War Memorial! 7 men joined regiments from the Empire; 5 died.

The others were spread around other regiments, including, interestingly, Roland Webster of the curiously named City of London Yeomanry - the battalion's adopted nickname of the 'Rough Riders' was taken from a US cavalry regiment that fought in the Spanish-American War. He had two addresses - Dorset Square, Marylebone and Hambleden Place where he died from wounds in 1915. At 47, he was the oldest of Our Men, and is buried in the Pheasants' Hill cemetery.

Having enlisted, each man had to be trained. The vast numbers of volunteers overwhelmed the resources of a regular army geared to the modest intakes of peacetime. Not only was accommodation at a premium (acres of tented camps were pitched), but what stocks there were of uniforms, weapons and equipment were rapidly absorbed. There existed no training organisation worthy of the name. With insufficient rifles and ammunition, hardly any artillery equipment, few horses and shortages of equipment and clothing, the new units could have undertaken little practical training, even if they had been fortunate enough to have sufficient instructors. They therefore spent most of their time at drill, physical training, route marching and digging. The trainers did their best. Men drilled with staves instead of rifles, did small arms training with rifles left over from the Boer War, and went all over the country on route marches, while artillerymen practiced gun drills with lengths of steel piping. The delays in the production of Vickers and Lewis guns prevented most battalions from beginning realistic machine-gun training for several months. In February 1915, men of the 6th Oxon & Bucks LI were still using a policeman's rattle to simulate the noise of a machine gun during mock battles.

It is sometimes asked why the army spent so much time in close-order drill, perfecting the art of turning to the right, left and about, marching up and down a parade square and performing complicated evolutions that appear to be more relevant to facing Napoleon at Waterloo than taking on the machine guns of the Germans. The answer is that the difference between an enthusiastic but untrained group of citizens and an army is discipline - the ability to react immediately and automatically under conditions of high stress. And the basis of that ability to react instantly is drill; square bashing was not a waste of time. Moreover, it had the effect of weeding out the unfit from the new battalions, and bringing about a noticeable improvement in physique and bearing in many of the men.

Few of the New Army battalions had seen a shot fired in anger by the time they were in action, although they had been in the army for several months, perhaps a year. During that time they were trained in trench warfare. We are fortunate to be able to inspect a set of training trenches right on our doorstep, in Pullingshill Wood, near Marlow, one of the best and most complete sets left in the UK. The 1,400m system of trenches was dug two metres deep and two metres wide, and was most likely constructed by the Grenadier Guards and the local people of Marlow. The Grenadier Guards, Welsh Guards, Royal Engineers and Royal Army Medical Corps, who were all based at the Bovingdon Green camp, are believed to have used the trenches during the two year period 1914-1915. On active service at the front a typical tour of duty would consist of four to seven days in the frontline trenches, the same in reserve and a week at rest. As many soldiers saw it, trench life was 90% routine and 10% terror. The 'rest' period offered some respite from enemy fire, but soldiers had to act as labourers, carrying forward to the trench lines the enormous amounts of materials needed for their maintenance and repair.

In March 2014, quite by accident, two sets of opposing trench systems, with a no man's land between, were found beneath heathland at the Ministry of Defence's Browndown site in Gosport, Hampshire. How many more are out there, I wonder?

However, it is one thing to train soldiers and quite another to furnish the officers and NCOs to lead them. Young men with the right background became officers and had to learn as they went along. It was a major incentive to a young officer to absorb a drill during an afternoon instruction parade if he knew that next morning he would have to teach the same thing to a batch of keen-witted and critical recruits!

Happily for the untrained officers and NCOs the men shared their desire to equip themselves as quickly as possible for active service. The extraordinary goodwill, which prevailed on both sides, enabled most units to complete their basic training much sooner than expected, considering the many obstacles they encountered.

By the spring of 1917 the British army was no longer a collection of enthusiastic amateurs, but a hardened, skilled and trained force, which got better and better as the war went on. That Britain had been able to create a mass citizen army almost from scratch within two and a half years was, in itself, a national achievement of colossal proportions.

Forty-six local men were killed in, or because of, the War; we have a record of only forty-three. A fifth fell in three black months which must have been awful in Hambleden – October 1916, and

August and October 1917; in each of these months three men died, some within days of each other. A chart of when Our Men died every six months during the War clearly demonstrates the pattern of fatalities:

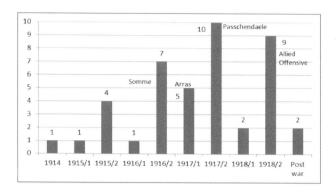

Until the Battle of the Somme, although it had experienced a fatality as early as 1 November 1914, Hambleden must have been thinking it had got off fairly lightly. Though no local man died on the first day of the Somme, 1 July 1916, when about one in forty of the nation's dead fell, six of Our Men were to die subsequently in that battle. Thereafter the church bells must have tolled solemnly at regular intervals. The Gray brothers, George and Harry, fighting for the Canadian forces, died within two days of each other in October 1916. Frederick Janes and Ernest Lyford, both in the Oxon & Bucks Light Infantry, died on the same day – 16 August, 1917. Frederick Plumridge from the Hyde and William Smith from Frieth, died within a day of each other in October 1917. These were grim days in our Parish, and illustrate the uneven pattern of fatalities. Parents, wives, brothers and sisters never knew when the dreaded telegram would arrive.

The wartime experience of Our Men is encapsulated in the lives and deaths of three men whose careers we have been able to follow. They are Brian Molloy, the first Hambleden man to perish and one of the few officers among Our Men, Arthur Gater who survived the Somme, and perhaps most poignantly, Alfred Dawson who died at home after fighting at Gallipoli and is buried in an unmarked grave in the cemetery at Pheasant's Hill.

Brian Charles Baskerville Molloy was born in Kensington. He was six when the family moved to Hambleden in 1882, from where he was sent to the Catholic Oratory School in Birmingham.

Life led at Hambleden was too leisurely for Brian, who from all accounts was a bit of a dasher and a terrier. By 1900, he had joined the Imperial Yeomanry (IY), and was in South Africa fighting the Boers. The original contingents of the IY were a motley collection of upper class toffs, including his friend Freddy Danvers Smith, who by that time had succeeded his father as head of the business. Both men had resigned a county Yeomanry commission, so desperate were they to get involved in the conflict. All that the men of the IY had in common was that they could ride; apart from this, standards of troops tended to vary considerably. Thankfully, they were held up at the Cape for long periods awaiting transport up country, which gave them time for much needed training and acclimatization.

Brian saw two significant actions in South Africa. The first was near Kimberley, by which time Brian had been promoted to the rank of temporary lieutenant. They defeated a rather strange force of foreign volunteers under the command of the aristocratic Frenchman Count de Villebois-Mareuil who was killed in the skirmish. In other words one group of strange aristocratic foreigners fighting another group of strange aristocratic foreigners, in a foreign country!

The second action took place in the small town of Lindley, was against real Boer fighters, and was not so successful. One officer and sixteen men were killed, and 400 were captured. Brian escaped, but was severely wounded. Subsequently the young men of the Yeomanry had a whale of a time riding hundreds of miles over the veldt, hunting wildlife, and rarely encountering any Boers. At the completion of the campaign, Brian was awarded the Queen's Medal with four clasps for his participation in the war.

In 1901, he returned to England, retired from the Yeomanry and joined the reserve of that Regiment in the same year, when he was also promoted Captain. As a civilian, he became a King's Foreign Service Messenger from 1901-13, hand-carrying secret and important documents to British consulates around the world.

Brian was a keen sportsman; he was a member of MCC, and played cricket for Oxfordshire, once, against Hertfordshire, in July 1902. He batted at number eight, but failed to trouble the scorers in either innings! He didn't get to bowl, and we don't know whether he actually ever touched the ball in the field! Oxfordshire were soundly beaten, and he never played for the county again. One may suspect that the only reason he played on this one occasion (probably because someone had dropped out at the last minute) was on the recommendation of his younger brother Maurice, who was a good player. We can imagine Brian digging out some old kit from the back of his wardrobe! We don't know whether either brother ever played for Hambleden.

Brian enjoyed a hectic social life in London, being a member of the St. James's and the Cavalry Clubs. However at the age of 34, he met May Pakenham, a wealthy widow from Yorkshire. They married and settled down in Half Moon Street, just off Piccadilly, where they had a daughter, Mary Elizabeth, in January 1912. Incidentally, in the census of 1911 Brian declined to reveal his occupation on the census form, perhaps because his occupation was somewhat confidential. Despite living in London, we know that Brian kept in close touch with Hambleden, for in March 1914 the Parish Magazine records a donation of a guinea from him to the Hambleden Nursing Association.

On the creation of the Territorial Force in April 1908, Brian's yeomanry reserve unit became the Queen's Own Oxfordshire Hussars (QOOH) or the 'Queer Objects On Horseback' – another regiment of toffs! One of the members of the QOOH was Winston Churchill, who had continued to perform roles in the regular army until 1900 when he left to go into politics but still found time to join the Hussars. In fact, he commanded the Henley Squadron between 1905 and 1913, and ensured high standards, which would serve the force well during the four years of active service they faced in France. It was at the instigation of Winston Churchill that the QOOH became the first territorial unit to see action in the War.

In 1909, every officer in the QOOH had been issued with secret mobilisation orders, and on 4 August 1914, telegrams were sent to them with the two words, 'We mobilise'. On 10 August, Brian's Banbury squadron entrained for Reading, having paraded at Banbury Cross and ridden off to the station to the cheers of the townspeople. From Reading, they moved to Norfolk, then to Churn, near Didcot.

Brian's story is now taken up by one of his fellow officers, the Hon. Arthur George Child Villiers, who kept a diary from their pre-embarkation days at Churn, and vividly recorded the story of Brian's last few days. He also gives a fascinating insight into a 'society' regiment.

Saturday, September 9th, 1914. Churn Farm, Churn.
I was awoken by Watkins at 3.30 saying that I had better get up as my regiment had been ordered abroad and was to leave at 9 a.m. I did not get up till five o'clock but was ready at the station at 8 with three horses, two servants, and all necessary kit -- I joined the Banbury Squadron. We went straight to the Southampton Docks and on board the Bellerophon. We sailed next morning -- some of our fellows were in cloth caps, others in their everyday breeches and it certainly seemed strange to go off with fellows of whom many had only left the plough a few days before --there were two red-headed fellows who had joined two days before we left and had on nothing military except a tunic -- however, Louis Egerton said that they were good chaps and I believe they are.

We were kept outside Dunkirk for 24 hours owing to a strong inshore wind -- however, we landed eventually safely and found billets all over the town. Gill and I were in the house of a builder where we were most comfortable. Charlie Nicholl was in the house of a demi-monde who wanted to do all she could for the soldats Anglais. Some of the men were put to sleep in the same room as four women, one of whom was sick on the floor. One of my fellows was put in the room of a man and his wife but I moved him. Another lot were billeted in the house of a lady who, when Val Fleming went to see her, showed him the corpse of a dead child -- she said that if they liked they could move it and stay there!

We stayed at Dunkirk until September 29th, drilling on the sands and dining at the Restaurant des Arcades. Eustace Fiennes left us to go in the Intelligence and Adrian Keith-Falconer became A.D.C. to the General of the Naval Division to which we were attached.

On our arrival at Dunkirk, we found Winston Churchill, F. E. Smith and Seely (formerly Minister of War) -- the two former had come by torpedo boat from England and the latter from the front --journeys no doubt of great value to the cause of Empire.

There has been a great movement of troops on this flank and there is no doubt that we shall shortly be in one of the biggest battles of the campaign -- some of our troops landed at Ostend have already been in a heavy action and we expect to move any day.

The French reservists are awful to look at -- absolutely hopeless in appearance but as one of the French officers said to Palmer -- they look all right from an aeroplane.

Dunkirk is full of Belgian motor cars with opulent refugees or soldiers.

October 28th. We moved on early in the morning and were told to go to St. Omer where are the H.Q. of Sir John French to whom we are bodyguard. Our daily routine of drill, shooting and exercise becomes rather monotonous and even the most unwarlike spirit like myself longs to be doing something.

There is plenty of society gossip -- the ancestral trees of many of those on the staff are long (or supposed to be) and there is a continual influx of politicians and members of the same kidney, some in khaki and some in plain clothes -- Lloyd George, Isaacs, Simon, Miss Violet Asquith, Duke of Marlborough, Hindlip, Ilchester, Arthur Lee, Seely, F. E. Smith, Neil Primrose, Eustace Fiennes, Geoffrey Howard, Pembroke, Percy, Castlereagh, etc., etc.

All of these have got some "job" -- F. E. and Neil had lunch with us today on their way to Merville, where the 27,000 Indians are concentrating. We have had several German Taubes over St. Omer but though they have dropped several bombs and been shot at they have given and received no damage.

I saw Colonel Lawrence yesterday who was over here arranging for the arrival of the 2nd Mounted Division

(Yeoman) which are to arrive probably at Le Havre next week. On October 30th (Friday) we received orders at 4.15 p.m. to proceed to Neuve Eglise -- we left at 7 p.m. and arrived after a very slow march at 7.30 a.m. at Neuve Eglise. We halted for nearly two hours at Neuve Eglise and then marched on towards Messines. When we were within half a mile of Messines we dismounted for action. At dusk we lined a ridge quite close to the town -- it was very cold, we had had practically no food and had no coats -- the men had been under fire all day both from rifles and shells and had marched 30 miles the previous night --rather a severe ordeal for untrained troops.

About II p.m. we marched to Messines. There was shrapnel bursting round us, houses in flames on all sides and a German gun firing down the street while we crept along the ditch up to our barricade. We passed 26 Germans who had just been captured by the regulars. We stayed waiting (very cold) until near 4 and then had some tea and biscuits and marched out to dig trenches. Having gone out about I mile with coats, spades, etc. we were told we could return and rest -- it was then nearly 7 --hardly had we returned when we were ordered to advance in open order towards Messines and keep back a German attack.

I was tired and how much worse the men must have been with rifles to carry. However, we spread out and advanced in one long line towards Messines. Then came the order to retire, which we did very slowly to a hedge about 600 yards in the rear. We lined this hedge, through which we could not see to shoot and which gave us no cover -- I was in the middle next to Warren and the bullets came all around us. It was a nasty position, as one could make no response. When at last Brian (by now a Major) gave us the order to retire we did so under heavy fire -- he was sitting up behind this hedge quite cool but he was shot through the head just after everyone but Warren had gone. It was very sad as it seemed so unnecessary.

His body was left on the battlefield as his troupe was under heavy fire. He was the first officer of the Regiment, and the first Hambleden man, to be killed in the War. He is remembered on the Hambleden

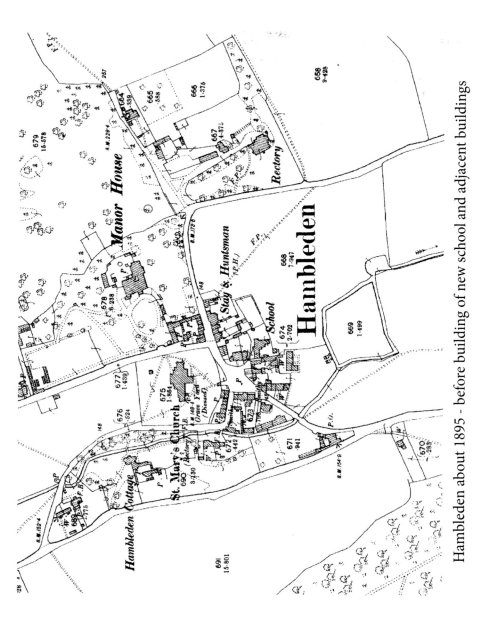

Hambleden about 1895 – before building of new school and adjacent buildings

The funeral of WH Smith as reported in the Huddersfield Daily Chronicle 17 October 1891.
Note the sketches of the church and the graveside.

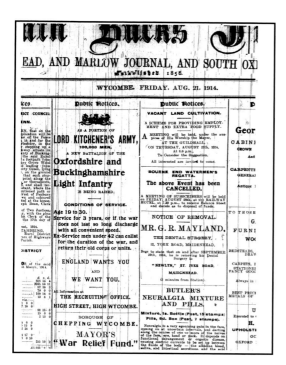

The front page of the
Bucks Free Press
21 August 1914.

Suffragettes distributing promotional literature at
Henley Regatta 1913. Note their elegance!

Recruiting poster for the Royal Naval Division - that may have attracted Our man Alfred Dawson.

Henley Regatta 1914.

Hambleden centre in 1910. Note two trees.

Hambleden Church circa 1910. Note the children sitting on the railings surrounding the garden on which the War Memorial now stands. The number is not a date - merely the number of the photo!

Greenlands circa 1910.

Frieth - PearTree Cottage & YewTree Inn 1914 Cottage occupied by
Mr Alfred Hussey;
Yew Tree Inn was the home of Our Man Frederick Leaver.

Freddie Danvers Smith,
2nd Viscount Hambleden,
in the uniform of
the Devon Yeomanry.

Field Workers at the turn of the century.

A Women's Institute float circa 1910.

A bunch of lads who were needed.

War Memorial. His name is also on the Memorial Board in the pavilion at Lords, and is recorded on the Menin Gate at Ypres. He left a wife (now twice widowed) and a daughter.

Brian's death is recorded in the official history of the Regiment 'The Oxfordshire Hussars in the Great War':

> *He was a great loss to the Regiment. His impetuous bravery, unchecked by any thought of danger was a valuable asset to untried troops in so desperate a conflict. He was a typical Irishman, and though at times may have been carried away by enthusiasm for the battle , he was a very gallant leader. His loss will be keenly felt.'*

Arthur Sidney Gater was born on 6 January 1892 at Yew Tree Cottage, Mill End, Hambleden, and was baptised in Hambleden Church on 7 February. His father, George, described himself as a labourer on the Baptism record; by the census of 1901 he had become 'head cattleman', and 'horseman on farm' by 1911. His mother, Ann, reveals in the 1911 census that she and George had been married 42 years, during which time she had borne eleven children, one of which had died. The last four of these children had been born between 1888 and 1892; in 1892 Ann was 45! Arthur was the youngest. By 1911 the family had moved to Coombe Terrace, by which time only two of her children were still at home, Arthur and his brother William who was two years older. Arthur also described himself in 1911 as a 'horseman on farm'; his brother was a packer at the flourmill at Mill End.

Arthur's name is on the Memorial Board in the Village Hall that commemorates some boys who had attended the school and who subsequently died in the War. We know, then, that he would have been able to read and write. While at the school, it is very likely that he would have known Our Man Alfred Dawson, who was only ten months younger, whose father was also a cattleman, and who lived relatively close by, in Burrow Farm.

Arthur joined the County of London Yeomanry, part of the prestigious 12th Battalion of the Middlesex Regiment (Duke of Cambridge's Own) on 19 April 1915 at the age of 23, some nine months after the War had started. Its members were intended only to serve for the duration of the war

Curiously, although he listed his address as Coombe Terrace on his enlistment papers, Arthur signed up at the Chelsea barracks. It may be that at the time he was staying with his elder sister, Agnes, who lived with her family in Tooting. We have no knowledge of his personal circumstances at the time, but as a horseman, one would have thought that he would be needed on the farm in Hambleden, especially as the need for agricultural output increased, as too did agricultural wages.

By early 1915, the recruitment boom of September 1914 had fizzled out, in part due to the widespread stories of congestion and discomfort at the depots and training centres resulting from the huge numbers that had enlisted since the outbreak of war. However, in November 1914, the Government went on the propaganda offensive; in January 1915 The Times recorded

> Posters appealing to recruits are to be seen on every hoarding, in most windows, in omnibuses, tramcars and commercial vans. The great base of Nelson's Column is covered with them. Their number and variety are remarkable. Everywhere Lord Kitchener sternly points a monstrously big finger, exclaiming 'I Want You'

By March 1915 it was estimated that some 20 million recruiting leaflets and some 2 million posters (including the famous pointing Kitchener) had been distributed. Public recruiting meetings were held up and down the country – in January 1915 it was reported that over 3,000 meetings had been held. Perhaps it was one of these that persuaded Arthur that the pressure to enlist outweighed his domestic responsibilities - or perhaps it was the news of the 58,000 casualties that had been incurred at the First Battle of Ypres, in October and November 1914, which had destroyed the BEF 'Old Contemptibles', or the 7,000 British and 4,200 Indian casualties incurred at the battle of Neuve Chapelle in March 1915. Or perhaps he did not want to face compulsory conscription that was rumoured to be about to be introduced (it was, the following January). We will never know.

The 12th Middlesex was part of the newly formed 18th (Eastern) Division of the Army. The Division was fortunate to be commanded by Major General Ivor Maxse, one of the ablest officers of his generation, a man of originality and drive, and a formidable personality. He was described by the military historian BH Liddell Hart as:

> 'short and dark, with a sallow complexion, small deep-set eyes, and a long drooping moustache, which gave him the look of a Tartar chief - all the more because the descriptive term 'a Tartar' so aptly fitted his manner in dealing with lazy or inefficient seniors and subordinates.....His fierce manner concealed a very warm heart, and he particularly liked people who showed that they were not afraid of him. He was always ready to encourage and make use of new ideas.'

While some officers were brought back from retirement to command units in the New Armies, others were rapidly promoted to fill the gaps. One such was Ivor Maxse who stepped up from the 1st Guards Brigade to command the 18th Division as a Major General. Following training - which Maxse personally oversaw – the Division spent the duration of the War in action on the Western Front, becoming one of the elite divisions of the British Army. It was commonly asserted that the Germans kept a list of the fifty most reliable British divisions – this included the Canadians, Australians, New Zealanders, South Africans, and the Guards; among the others was the 18th. There is no evidence that such a list existed, but the soldiers believed it, and were proud to be on it. The historian Jonathan Nicholls described them as 'probably the best fighting division possessed by the British Army in September 1916'.

One of the foundations on which its reputation was built was the use of the machine gun. Unlike the mistrust with which the Lewis gun was viewed in some sections of the Army, Maxse was a firm advocate of the machine gun, and used his influence to ensure that it formed the basis of infantry training in his Division, and later in 1918, when he became Inspector General of Training, in the Army as a whole. Through his energies, by the end of the War, the infantry battalion had been wholly transformed.

Having enlisted, Arthur moved to Colchester for training. Uniforms and weapons were in short supply. Often the recruits had to train in the civilian clothes in which they had enlisted, and which were soon reduced to rags by the rigours of training. In the 18th Division at Colchester, route marches began with the order: 'Men without boots on the right, men with worn out trousers to the left.' An artillery officer within the Division later described how his unit drilled with wooden guns and shells:

> *If the gun was loaded smartly, the wooden shell was sent several feet from the muzzle....by the impetus given to it by the No 4! We also began to learn field movements. Six men marched with a red flag representing a gun team, and six men marched with a white flag pretending to be a wagon team.*

In May, Arthur moved to Codford for final training, to be hardened for active service before crossing to France – for example, a two-night exercise in the Codford trenches:

> *All the irritating restrictions were enforced; no movement except under cover; no field kitchens or rations allowed up before dark; communications by telephone; and the trenches improved or dug during the hours of darkness.*

Established in somewhat straggling fashion among the bleak, bare, undulating downs of Salisbury Plains, Codford camp was not popular for its surroundings or its exterior attractions. The camp was in a field bounded by a stream on three sides. Warnings from local residents that that the field was often flooded and used for skating in winter were ignored; when it was not freezing, after heavy rains the field would be a quagmire (Arthur probably felt at home!)

Inevitably, the growth of such camps transformed the appearance of the countryside. Less than a mile from the camp lay the little old-fashioned Wiltshire village from which the camp derived its name - the only oasis of interest in the midst of a drab environment. The Brigade Chaplain recorded of Codford in the summer of 1915:

The two villages of Codford St Mary and St Peter, which joined together could scarcely muster 700 souls, find themselves changed........The old sleepy village is half filled with horrid booths and shanties, where tobacco, hosiery, and a thousand odds and ends can be bought for an increased cost, for the owner of the property has asked £1 a week in rent for a glorified cupboard which now constitutes a shop. A cottage lets its front parlour to a bank, and the wax fruit with the family Bible have gone, and money bags replace the old institutions....

Perhaps fortunately, they did not stay long at Codford; they proceeded to France on the 26 July 1915 landing at Le Havre, where training continued. Arthur did not see action until July 1916, when his unit was involved in the Battle of the Somme. Up to that point, his life was a continual round of battle and attack training, path building, hut improvement, moving from billets in one indistinguishable French village only to tramp to another in apparently aimless circles. However, the infantry were glad on the whole to be on the move. They had been at the front for many months, in trenches that graduated from quiet to lively, and had become hardened to discomfort and cautiously blasé under shellfire; but they had not been required to go 'over the top' in a major battle.

Life may have seemed menial and often hard, but it served to provide the social cohesion that was one of the most important characteristics of the New Armies. The men ate, slept and worked in the sections and platoons in which they were to fight. The officers not only knew their men by sight and name, and each individual's level of proficiency, but also knew many of the details of their private affairs, and in some cases even their families. Thus, whatever the weaknesses of their training, there was an understanding and sympathy between all ranks that was to stand them in good stead when they came to be tested in the crucible of battle.

And into the crucible they went! The New Army's first encounter with all-out war was on the Somme, and given that they were a citizen army, lacking in experience, training and equipment, the result was inevitably shocking. The Battle of the Somme has come to epitomise the horror and hardship of the War. Visiting the battlefields today one might wonder why it was ever selected. There were no major communication lines or industrial complexes behind the German lines, and the British found themselves fighting up a long and steep ridge, whose lower slopes were dotted with coppices and fortified villages, against some of the strongest positions on the Western Front.

To ensure a rapid advance, Allied artillery pounded German lines for a week before the attack, firing 1.6 million shells. British commanders were so confident they ordered their troops to walk slowly towards the German lines. Once they had been seized, cavalry units would pour through to pursue the fleeing Germans. However, unconcealed preparations for the assault and the weeklong bombardment gave the Germans clear warning. Their trenches were heavily fortified and, furthermore, many of the British shells failed to explode. When the bombardment began, the Germans simply moved underground and waited.

Final preparations of training and planning were made by the British infantry during the days of the preparatory bombardment. On 30 June, messages of encouragement were sent to the men by their commanders. Field services were held in the rear areas by the padres and chaplains. Some units held parades with bands playing. Equipment was cleaned and checked. Letters were written. Each man collected his ammunition. Kit to be carried into battle was handed out. The troops fell in to their units and prepared for the march that night into the Assembly Trenches in the forward area. Between 02.00 hours and 05.15 hours, thousands of British troops made their way on a moonless, but clear night along pre-prepared routes to the forward lines to be in position and ready for Zero Hour at 07.30 on 1 July.

What followed was a massacre – though not for the 18th Division. The artillery had done their job in their sector – there was virtually no barbed wire defence left after the preceding artillery bombardment, and the German troops were not able to man all their parapets when the British shellfire lifted. The attack itself began with the detonation of a series of 17 mines, the first of which actually went off at 07:20. The detonation of this mine, the Hawthorn Crater, remains visible to this day. The fall-out from the mines caused minor casualties as far back as the British second trench!

Maxse had had the bright idea of hiding his division in no man's land in shallow trenches and tunnels before the battle was joined, and then having them closely follow the creeping barrage towards the German line. The advance of the lead units was so quick it actually ran into the British barrage and had to wait for the planned 'lift' at 07.45 before they could press on. However, they did not have things their own way; it was not until 17.15 that their objective, Montauban, was taken. A small enemy counterattack was beaten off at 21.30. The Division's losses on the day amounted to over 6,100 officers and men. But the carnage was not over; enemy shellfire falling on Montauban, the village and the defences and on the old no man's land, intensified and stayed heavy, causing many casualties and making relief and re-supply very problematic for the tired units now holding the new positions. But hold they did, and Arthur was part of one of the few divisions that achieved all its objectives of first day of the Battle of the Somme.

Of the 120,000 British troops taking part on that day, about 57,000 became casualties and over 19,000 died.

Thereafter the battle got bogged down, the British suffering another 82,000 casualties in dozens of minor operations until the end of September. Arthur's regiment was involved in many of them – at Bazentin Ridge in which the Division captured Trones Wood; at Delville Wood in which the Division supported the South African Brigade in taking and holding the position under heavy shelling; at Thiepval Ridge, in which the British took the dominating position at the top end of the ridge; the battle of the Ancre Heights in which the Division played a part in the capture of the German defence positions at Schwaben Redoubt and Regina Trench. Limited attacks continued in worsening weather until the final battle of the Ancre in mid-November.

It was in the Thiepval Heights operation on 26 September that a member of the 12th Middlesex won a Victoria Cross. 20-year-old Private Robert Ryder's company was held up by heavy rifle fire and all his officers had become casualties. For want of leadership the attack was flagging when Private Ryder, realising the situation and without a moment's thought for his own safety dashed, absolutely alone, at the enemy trench and by skilful handling of his Lewis gun succeeded in clearing the trench. This very gallant act inspired his comrades, made the subsequent advance possible and turned what could have been failure into success.

After the close of the Battle of the Somme in November 1916, the men on the Western Front dug in for the coming winter.

It was to be the last winter that Arthur would see.

During the rest of 1916 and early January 1917, military operations by both sides were mostly restricted to survival in the rain, snow, fog, mud fields, waterlogged trenches and shell-holes. It turned out to be exceptionally cold. All those who lived through that winter had memories of the bitterly freezing conditions.

But before the freeze, it rained! The winter we have just experienced (2013-14) has been the wettest in living memory, so we know all about heavy rain, and so may have some idea of what conditions were like. In 1916-17 rain flooded the trenches; for weeks men were up to the thighs in mud. Any movement to or from the front line was made hazardous by the shell holes, many of which were filled up with muddy clay - Arthur would have felt at home! Roddy Baird's grandfather was a Brigadier General with the 75th Infantry Brigade on the Western Front, and noted in his diary that men could and did drown in the deep, muddy craters. He wrote

> *The carrying parties had to contend with the greatest difficulties in having to move across a shellpot zone, in thick slime and mud, and under constant shell fire.*

And when they froze, the trenches would disintegrate, so that the front line was not a continuous trench but more a collection of little holes, or a series of sludge-filled ditches. When the ground was frozen solid digging was impossible. However, the frozen ground did have some benefits – one soldier recorded a lucky escape in his diary:

> *The ground was so hard that a shell just glisséed on the surface. It struck within about a yard (!) to the right-hand side of me as I was walking and then went on and in the air, about 150 yards beyond, it burst. Now, if that had been soft I'd have had it.* (My exclamation mark.)

If the icy weather made life during the day miserable, the drop in temperature at night was even worse. The men attempted to alleviate the cold with thick woollen underwear and woollen shirts, a cardigan or a pullover beneath their uniform. On top of that, they had an overcoat. Gauntlets and sheepskin coats, to be worn fleece outward, were issued only to the troops who were manning the front line. Those behind the front line were issued woollen gloves and a woollen scarf which acted as a cover under the helmet.

Despite the extra layers, many of the men still fell victim to frostbite and trench foot, which made their feet swell up when they took their boots off, so they were unable to put them back on. It was terribly painful; toes and even feet were lost.

The bitter cold also froze clothing, blankets, food and drink. One soldier remembered

> ...in the front line, I can remember we weren't allowed to have a brazier because it weren't far away from the enemy and therefore we couldn't brew up tea. But we used to have tea sent up to us, up the communication trench. Well a communication trench can be as much as three quarters of a mile long. It used to start off in a huge dixie, two men would carry it like a stretcher. It would start off boiling hot; by the time it got to us in the front line, there was ice on the top it was so cold.

Water bottles were frozen stiff; soldiers had to cut them in half, and suck the ice out. They would go down to the River Ancre at night with pick-axes to try to get through to the water, but rarely succeeded.

At Christmas, a ration of Christmas pudding and extra rum was distributed, and the officers brought some wine among the troops.

For British sapper George Clayton, the simple task of shaving was made almost impossible by the sub-zero temperatures:

> You could get a handful of snow and put it into one of them empty Capstan tins, you know we used to get tins of Capstan, had 60 cigarettes, it was just about like a milk thing. And you could warm your snow in there to get water underneath a

candle then you had some warm water when the snow melted.
Have a shave and by the time you were shaved – they issued us
with cut throat razors there wasn't any safeties in them days –
but by the time you were shaved, the water was frozen again to
ice. And you had to melt the water that you'd left your lather
brush in before you could get it out! It was a block of ice again!

Arthur would have spent many days in the trenches. In France, the chalky soil, with which he would have been familiar, lent itself well to deep trenches, with high parapets built up with sandbags giving some cover against sniping. Soldiers would create a 'funk hole' in which to live by scraping into a wall, and lining it with rubber capes. Wet weather was universally hated, causing flooding and balls of chalk to cling to soldiers' feet. For much of the time, trench life was a monotonous regime, though if winter was grim, it was perhaps compensated for by spring when the soil was ablaze with poppies and cornflowers, and larks, unaccountably still resident, would hover, trilling in the sky.

The 18th Division was back in action long before spring. It was involved in operations on the River Ancre between January and March 1917, specifically in the actions of Miraumont in February and the capture of Irles in early March.

In March 1917, the German armies on the Somme carried out a strategic withdrawal, destroying everything on the ground that they left: flattening villages, poisoning wells, cutting down trees, blowing craters on roads and crossroads, booby-trapping ruins and dugouts. The withdrawal was to an immensely more powerful and shorter line, positioned to take every tactical advantage of ground. A cautious pursuit began – the Arras offensive. It was in an action as part of this operation, on 3 May, in the small farming village of Chérisy, some 9 miles southeast of Arras, that Arthur Gater was killed. A group of the 12th Middlesex got into the village itself and congregated in the open barn by the crossroads, only to be machine gunned, bombed and bayonetted almost to extinction. The German counter-attack forced their line back to its starting position, and the attack was called off the following day after incurring heavy casualties - 25 killed; 114 wounded and 173 missing.

Arthur's body was never found – he was one of those reported as missing. As well as on the Hambleden War memorial, he is commemorated on the Arras Memorial situated in the War Graves Cemetery in Arras.

He was entitled to Victory and War Medals; these were received by his father in 1919, no doubt with great pride and sadness.

Alfred John Dawson was born on 27 November 1892, one of nine children, and baptised in the Parish Church on 5 February the following year. His family were living at the time at Burrows Farm, where his father was a farm labourer, though subsequently they moved to Mill End Farm, then owned by Charles Scott Murray, and now farmed by Oliver Bowden. Alfred began his schooling in the building that is now the Village Hall, but would have spent more time at the 'new school' (now confusingly called the 'old school') which was built in 1897. Like many children at the time, his attendance may well have been erratic, depending on what needed to be done on the farm and the state of his health – we know that he was off school in February 1902 when diphtheria broke out in the Dawson household. However, he must have showed some promise, for he was commended in the Headmaster's Log on three separate occasions. In any case, he would have left at the age of thirteen.

The whole family would have surely enjoyed the Henley Show which took place at the farm in 1906, and thirteen year old Alfred and his father would have been very busy as part of the organising team.

His father, John, had become a cowman, but who sadly was to meet a terrible death in 1937, when he was gored by a bull.........at the age of 76! His mother, Matilda, was a tiny, indomitable woman who became caretaker of the Museum in 1924, where she lived until she retired. After retirement, she lived till her death at the age of 102 at the cottage 88 Hambleden. Eric, Alfred's great nephew, tells me that she was still walking into Henley at the age of 80, and still collecting large bundles of firewood from the woods above the school. A photo of her can be found in Charles Gray's book 'Born on Chiltern Slopes'.

Alfred had strong genes!

We know from the Census that Alfred was still living at Mill

End in 1911 where he is described as a gardener, but soon after he took himself off to Pyrford in Surrey where he found work, also as a gardener. Interestingly, in the 1911 Census, the family were boarding a prison warder and his wife.

It was from Pyrford that Alfred joined the Royal Naval Division (RND) at the outbreak of the war. Why the navy for a man who had likely never seen the sea? I suspect it was a combination wanting to do something different and the hope that he might see a bit of the world.

If he was hoping to spend the War at sea, he was sadly mistaken. At the declaration of the war so many recruits enlisted in the navy that there was a surplus of some 20-30,000 men who could not find jobs on any ship of war. As the war would be conducted mainly on land, there was an obvious solution; it was Churchill who decided to use the men to augment the army for operations on land – hence its nickname as 'Winston's Little Army'.

Support the army it might have done, but the RND retained the great naval traditions, even while on land. They flew the White Ensign, used bells to signal time, wore beards, used naval language (including 'going ashore' and 'coming on board'), continued to use naval ranks rather than army equivalents and sat during the toast for the King's health. Attempts to convert the RND to conform to army practices were tried but were generally unsuccessful as the following verses may illustrate. They were aimed at Major General Cameron Shute, appointed CO of the RND in October 1916. General Shute had an intense dislike for the unconventional 'nautical' traditions of the division and made numerous unpopular attempts to stamp them out. Following a particularly critical inspection of the trenches, an officer of the division, one Sub-Lieutenant A. P. Herbert summed up the slightly subversive mood of the men of the RND – a mood that no doubt appealed to Alfred:

The General inspecting the trenches
Exclaimed with a horrified shout
'I refuse to command a division
Which leaves its excreta about.'

But nobody took any notice
No one was prepared to refute,
That the presence of shit was congenial
Compared to the presence of Shute.

And certain responsible critics
Made haste to reply to his words
Observing that his staff advisors
Consisted entirely of turds.

For shit may be shot at odd corners
And paper supplied there to suit,
But a shit would be shot without mourners
If somebody shot that shit Shute.

The RND began training for overseas service in mid-August, and the naval battalions were assembled in Kent towards the end of the month finally being brought together at Crystal Palace in September 1914. Training was slow; resources were scarce in any case, and most resources were channelled for the rapid expansion of the Army. Some ratings had not even been issued with field equipment or khaki uniforms before being embarked for overseas service. Rifles were drawn from Royal Navy stockpiles, and only arrived at the end of September; these were older charger-loading Lee Enfields rather than the more modern short magazine Lee-Enfields issued to the Army. The division as a whole was not provided with support units - there were no medical, artillery, or engineer units - and consisted solely of lightly-equipped infantry.

In February 1915 the Division was shipped to Egypt prior to serving in the Battle of Gallipoli. Casualties before the hostilities included officer and poet, Rupert Brooke, who developed sepsis from an infected mosquito bite, and who subsequently died at sea on 23 April. Who knows, Alfred may have attended his burial, on a hilltop on the Greek island of Skyros. This was their final stop before they were tasked to support the Australian and New Zealand forces at Gallipoli.

Conditions on Gallipoli defy description, and one can only

imagine the effect they had on a young man from Hambleden. The terrain and close fighting did not allow for the dead to be buried. Flies and other vermin flourished in the heat, which caused epidemic sickness. Of the 213,000 British casualties on Gallipoli, 145,000 were due to sickness, the chief causes being dysentery, diarrhoea, and enteric fever. Others suffered from disease, such as Hepatitis A, contracted from contaminated food or water.

Although Alfred survived the battle, he contracted some disease, and was invalided back to Britain. Eric remembers being told that he had something wrong with his chest. He never recovered, and died at his home in Pyrford on 1 December 1915. His body was moved to Hambleden, possibly at the expense of Mr Scott Murray, where it was buried anonymously in an unmarked grave in the Pheasants' Hill cemetery on 9 December 1915.

Perhaps we should leave the last word to Rupert Brooke. The lines seem to sum up the sentiments that may have passed through the minds of Our Men as they prepared for battle.

The Soldier (1914)

IF I should die, think only this of me;
  That there's some corner of a foreign field
That is for ever England. There shall be
  In that rich earth a richer dust concealed;
A dust whom England bore, shaped, made aware,
  Gave, once, her flowers to love, her ways to roam,
A body of England's breathing English air,
  Washed by the rivers, blest by suns of home.

And think, this heart, all evil shed away,
  A pulse in the eternal mind, no less
    Gives somewhere back the thoughts by England given;
Her sights and sounds; dreams happy as her day;
  And laughter, learnt of friends; and gentleness,
    In hearts at peace, under an English heaven.

William Barlow

Personal

Born: Jul-Sep 1889   in Beaconsfield

Baptised: 28/09/1889 Beaconsfield

Occupation: Farmer

Address: The Royal Oak, Frieth

Family

Married Status: single

Mother: Emily

Father: Thomas

Father's occupation:

Parents Address:

Military

Enlisted: Marlow

Regiment: Gloucestershire 8 Btn

Rank: Private 27730

Died: Killed in Action 11 November 1916   Aged:27

Place of death: Battle of Ancre Heights

Buried:

Memorial: Thiepval Memorial, Somme; Pier & Face
                      5A & 5B

Additional Information

For most of his life William lived with his uncle, Edmund Barlow, who was publican at the Royal Oak in Frieth William joined up in 1916 (Parish Magazine: May 1916)

The Parish Magazine of December 1916 carries a notice of William's death

Cecil Batchelor

Personal

Born: Jul-Sep 1894   in Medmenham

Baptised:

Occupation: Post Office Telegraph Messenger

Address: Ridge Wood Cottage, Hambleden

Family

Married Status: single

Mother: Alice Marie

Father: George

Father's occupation: Gamekeeper

Parents Address: Ivy Cottage/Ridge Wood Cottage,
                                     Greenlands

Military

Enlisted: Leicester 09/10/1914

Regiment: Leicestershire 1/4 Btn

Rank: Private 200727

Died: Killed in Action 08 June 1917   Aged:22

Place of death: Messines Ridge

Buried: Pas de Calais

Memorial: Arras Memorial, Pas de Calais, Bay 5

Additional Information

Brother of Ernest.

Pte. Batchelor was instantly killed while attending an officer who was wounded in fierce fighting on June 9th. (South Bucks Press: 22/06/1917)

Pte. Batchelor joined the Leicester Regiment in October 1914. In June 1916 he was sent to hospital in England, but returned to France in December last. He was one of three brothers, all of whom voluntarily enlisted. (South Bucks Press: 22/06/1917)

Ernest Batchelor

Personal
  Born: 01/06/1898   in Hambleden
  Baptised: 07/08/1898 Hambleden
  Occupation: Schoolboy
  Address: Ridge Wood Cottage, Hambleden

Family
  Married Status: single
  Mother: Alice Marie
  Father: George
  Father's occupation: Gamekeeper
  Parents Address: Ivy Cottage/Ridge Wood Cottage,
                Greenlands

Military
  Enlisted: Oxford
  Regiment: Kings Royal Rifles 18 Btn
  Rank: Lance Corporal 12400
  Died: Killed in Action 21 September 1917   Aged:19
  Place of death: Menin Rd Ridge
  Buried: Hooge Crater Cemetery, Ieper, XX.H.6
  Memorial:

Additional Information

Brother of Cecil.

[The] Company Officer writes: "... Lce.-Corpl. E. Batchelor was killed in action on the 20th inst. whilst leading his section with great gallantry against a strong enemy position. He was one of the smartest N.C.O.s in the Company, and a man in whom I had great confidence, and was very popular with all the N.C.O.s and men, always doing his duty with great coolness and devotion. He died a hero, fighting for home, King, country, and freedom". Further particulars show that this fine soldier died without pain, and was buried behind the British lines. The brave fellow enlisted at the age of seventeen, and had just completed his nineteenth year at the time of his death. He was a member of the Hambleden Troop of Boy Scouts from its beginning, eight years ago, until the time of his enlistment. He was most popular with his fellow Scouts, and proved himself a splendid shot with a rifle. He gained distinction in marksmanship in the Army, qualified as a bomber, and crossing to France less than four months ago, gained promotion to N.C.O.'s rank. (South Bucks Press 05/10/1917).

Sidney Bond

Personal
    Born: 14/01/1893   in Frieth
    Baptised: 05/03/1893 Frieth
    Occupation: Servant (Hall Boy)
    Address: Wormseley, Stokenchurch

Family
    Married Status: single
    Mother: Annie
    Father: Frederick
    Father's occupation: Wood-turner in Chair Factory
    Parents Address: Frieth

Military
    Enlisted: High Wycombe
    Regiment: Gloucestershire 10 Btn
    Rank: Private 15612
    Died: Killed in Action 25 September 1915   Aged:22
    Place of death: Loos Sector
    Buried:
    Memorial: Loos Memorial, Pas de Calais, Panel 60 & 64

Additional Information

Brother of Wilfred.

First young man from Frieth to be killed (Parish Magazine: 11/1917).

"...The first news his parents received was that he was missing, from a private source, and then that he was killed, from a comrade who assisted to bury him, and later on this sad intelligence was confirmed by official information from the War Office... he was always of a bright and cheerful disposition and respected by all with whom he came in contact. His comrades write of him that he was one of the best of pals, and they are deeply grieved at their loss. Also his captain, to whom he was servant for nearly a year before going to the Front, writes that he is extremely sorry, as he was deeply attached to him. The late Private Bond was well known in Stokenchurch, and also in the Wycombe and District Cricket League circles, as he had assisted Stokenchurch in many of their League fixtures. His services were much sought after, being a good bowler, as well as bat, and many are sorry to hear of his death. At one time he was in the service of Mr. Fane, of Wormesley, as under servant, and for five years he enjoyed the high esteem of his employer." (South Bucks Press, 19/11/1915)

Wilfred Bond

Personal

Born: Apr-Jun 1898 in Frieth

Baptised:

Occupation: schoolboy

Address: living with parents

Family

Married Status: single

Mother: Annie

Father: Frederick

Father's occupation: Wood-turner in Chair Factory

Parents Address: Frieth

Military

Enlisted: High Wycombe

Regiment: Oxon & Bucks Light Infantry 2nd/4th
                     Btn

Rank: 202735

Died: Killed in Action 25 August 1918   Aged:20

Place of death: Neuf Berquin

Buried: Merville Communal Cemetery Extension,
                     Nord, IV.C.1

Memorial:

Additional Information

Awarded Military Medal (awarded to ranks below a confirmed Warrant Officer for acts of bravery in combat)

"Wilfred Bond, whose stay at home is all too short, is the first Frieth man, I believe, to get the Military Medal, and the first Frieth man to sign the C.E.M.S. War Roll - the Roll of Jesus Christ." (Parish Magazine for Mar 1918)

"The gallant soldier has only been in France a short time, and his acquaintances are delighted that he has so soon gained distinction." (also mentions that he was a member of the Fox Patrol of the Boy Scouts) (South Bucks Press, 05/10/1917)

111

Charles Buckell

Personal
    Born: in
    Baptised:
    Occupation:
    Address:

Family
    Married Status:
    Mother:
    Father:
    Father's occupation:
    Parents Address:

Military
    Enlisted:
    Regiment:
    Rank:
    Died: Aged:
    Place of death:
    Buried:
    Memorial:

Additional Information
No information about this person has been found.

Percy Clinkard

Personal

Born: Apr-Jun 1888   in   Cadmore End, Fingest

Baptised:

Occupation: Soldier 2nd Btn Gloucesters

Address: Malta

Family

Married Status: single

Mother: Mary Ann

Father: James W.

Father's occupation: labourer with District Council

Parents Address: Moors End, Frieth

Military

Enlisted: Caversham

Regiment: Gloucestershire 7 Btn

Rank: Private 8590

Died: Died of Wounds 11 December 1915   Aged:27

Place of death: Gallipoli

Buried: Pieta Military Cemetery, Malta, C.I.4

Memorial:

Additional Information

"... Percy Thomas Clinkard, youngest son of Mr and Mrs Clinkard of Moor End, joined the Army some nine years ago, at the age of 18. Six of these years were served abroad. He was stationed with his Regiment - the Gloucesters - in China when the War broke out. Three months later he arrived home, with five days leave before proceeding to the Front. In January of this year he was sent to Gravesend Hospital with frozen feet, and there contracted scarlet fever, which necessitated many months convalescence in a sanatorium. Finally, after a short stay at home, he returned to the Front on November 13th, from which date no further news was received from him till an official message from the base hospital at Malta announced the sad news of his death from abdominal wounds." (South Bucks Press, 31/12/1915)

"Frieth suffered the first loss of life in Sidney Bond and has now been called to give a second in Percy Clinkard of the 2nd Gloucesters (temporarily attached to the 7th) who died of wounds received at the Dardanelles, in a hospital in Malta." (Parish Magazine, Jan 1916)

Alfred Coker

Personal

Born: Jul-Sep 1900   in Skirmett

Baptised:

Occupation: Schoolboy

Address: Skirmett

Family

Married Status: single

Mother: Kate Eva

Father: James William

Father's occupation: Waggoner in Flour Mill

Parents Address: Chapel House, Skirmett

Military

Enlisted: Aylesbury

Regiment: Prince Albert's (Somerset Light Infantry)
1st Btn

Rank: Private 30792

Died: Killed in Action 03 September 1918   Aged:18

Place of death: Drocourt-Queant

Buried:

Memorial: Vis-en-Artois Memorial, Pas de Calais,
Panel 4

Additional Information

William Collison

Personal

Born: Jan-Mar 1896 in Hambleden

Baptised:

Occupation: Game Keeper's Assistant

Address: living with parents

Family

Married Status: single

Mother: Sarah Elizabeth

Father: George Edward

Father's occupation: head game keeper

Parents Address: Burrough Farm, Hambleden

Military

Enlisted: Reading

Regiment: East Kent (The Buffs) 2nd Btn

Rank: Private G/6535

Died: Killed in Action 28 September 1915   Aged:19

Place of death: Loos

Buried:

Memorial: Loos Memorial, Pas de Calais, Panel 15 to 19

Additional Information

William John Collison, known as Jack.

"Mr. Collison of Borough, has received official intimation that his elder son, Pte. W. Collison was killed in the battle of Loos on Sept. 28th 1915. He was reported missing last autumn, and nothing could be heard of him till last Saturday, when the information given above came to hand. Pte. Collison joined the Dragoon Guards soon after the outbreak of War, but was afterwards transferred to the Buffs (East Kent Regiment). Everybody who knew him ("Jack") liked him, and will be sorry to know that now there can be no hope of his return." (South Bucks Press, 01/12/1916)

William Cook

Personal
Born: 06/09/1886   in Hambleden
Baptised: 10/10/1886 Hambleden
Occupation: farm labourer
Address: unknown

Family
Married Status: presumed single
Mother: Rose
Father: Stephen
Father's occupation: head carter on farm
Parents Address: Huttons, Hambleden

Military
Enlisted: Reading
Regiment: Gloucestershire 8 Btn
Rank: Private 25628
Died: Killed in Action 30 July 1916   Aged: 29
Place of death:
Buried: Caterpillar Valley Cemetery, Lonqueval, Somme, VI.D.29

Memorial:

Additional Information

George Cutler

Personal
Born: Apr-Jun 1891 in Frieth
Baptised: 22/05/1891   Lane End
Occupation: chauffeur
Address: Steyning, Hove, Sussex
Family
Married Status: single
Mother: Margaret Jane (nee Brazier)
Father: George Edwin
Father's occupation: wheelwright
Parents Address: Frieth
Military
Enlisted: Brandon, Manitoba
Regiment: Canadian Mounted Rifles 1st Btn
                       (Saskatchewan Regiment)
Rank: Private 424721
Died: Died   09 April 1917   Aged:29
Place of death: Vimy Ridge
Buried: Ecoivres Military Cemetery, Mont-St.Eloi,
                       Pas de Calais, V.D.27

Memorial:

Additional Information
Left Liverpool on 31 May 1913 for Quebec aboard the Allan Line
steamer 'Corsican'.

Robert George Cutler on enlistment papers with date of birth given
as 24 Jan 1892. This is at odds with the age at death of 29 given by
the Commonwealth War Graves Commission; which would give
the year of birth as c. 1888. On the 1901 Census, age is given as 10
(giving year of birth as c. 1891). The birth of a Robert George Cutler
is registered at Wycombe for Apr-Jun 1891.

The Parish Magazine for May 1917 states: "We were very sorry to
learn of the death of Mr. and Mrs. Cutler's son - George - killed in

action out in France. It appears that he met his death as he was being carried wounded out of action."

Alfred Dawson

Personal
Born: 27/11/1892   in Hambleden
Baptised: 05/02/1893 Hambleden
Occupation: Gardener
Address: Mill End

Family
Married Status: single
Mother: Eliza Matilda
Father: John
Father's occupation: farm labourer
Parents Address: Mill End

Military
Enlisted:
Regiment: Royal Naval Division
Rank: Ordinary Seaman Z/543
Died: Died at home   01 December 1915   Aged:23
Place of death: Pyrford, Surrey
Buried: St. Mary, Churchyard, Hambleden
Memorial:

Additional Information

Death from disease contracted whilst serving at Gallipoli.
Died while working as gardener at Pyrford Court Gardens, Surrey.
Buried in Hambleden 9 Dec 1915.
For more information, see main text.

Frank Deane

Personal

    Born: Oct-Dec 1897 in Skirmett

    Baptised:

    Occupation: Schoolboy

    Address: Pheasants Hill

Family

    Married Status: single

    Mother: Annie

    Father: William

    Father's occupation: woodman on estate

    Parents Address: Pheasant's Hill

Military

    Enlisted: Aylesbury

    Regiment: Royal Warwickshire 2nd Btn

    Rank: Private 30006

    Died: Died of Wounds 30 December 1918   Aged:21

    Place of death:

    Buried: Perreuse Chateau Franco British National
                      Cemetery, I.C.48

    Memorial:

Additional Information

Formerly Private 21049 in the Oxon & Bucks Light Infantry

Arthur Edwards

Personal

Born: Apr-Jun 1899 in Frieth, Hambleden

Baptised: not in register

Occupation: schoolboy

Address: living with parents

Family

Married Status: single

Mother: Emma Louisa

Father: George

Father's occupation: carter on farm

Parents Address: Frieth

Military

Enlisted: Oxford

Regiment: Royal Irish Rifles 2nd Btn

Rank: Corporal 54206

Died: Died of Wounds 08 August 1918   Aged:19

Place of death:

Buried: Arneke British Cemetery, III.C.6

Memorial:

Additional Information

Formerly Private 9334 in the Rifle Brigade

"It is with deep sorrow that we heard the sad news that Arthur Edwards had died of wounds out in France. There is not many an English lad who has spent the years from his 15th birthday - as he did - fighting for his country with one brief spell of respite." (Parish Magazine, Sep 1918)

Arthur Gater

Personal

Born: 16/01/1892   in Hambleden

Baptised: 07/02/1892   Hambleden

Occupation: Horseman on farm

Address: Coombe Terrace

Family

Married Status:

Mother: Anne

Father: George William

Father's occupation: head carter on farm

Parents Address: Coombe Terrace, Hambleden

Military

Enlisted: Chelsea, 19/04/1915

Regiment: Middlesex Regiment 12th Btn

Rank: Private G/40711

Died: Killed in Action 03 May 1917   Aged:25

Place of death: Cherisy, France

Buried:

Memorial: Arras Memorial, Pas de Calais, Bay 7

Additional Information

Formerly Private 3987 County of London Yeomanry

"...The officer commanding the gallant soldier's company (Middlesex Regiment) has written as follows: - "Dear Mr. Gater, - I am afraid that I have very bad news to break to you in this letter. Your son, Pte. Gater, was killed in action on the morning of May 3rd. I cannot tell you how sorry I am to have to write you this letter. Your son was a very gallant soldier. He was killed during an advance and died instantly..." (South Bucks Press, 18/05/1917)

For more information, see main text.

Thomas Gearing

Personal

Born: Jan-Mar 1879 in Farringdon, Berks.

Baptised:

Occupation: Carter on Farm

Address: Rockwell End, Hambleden

Family

Married Status: married: Agnes Jane Moore Oct-Dec 1908
in Farringdon

Mother: Mary

Father: George

Father's occupation: cowman on farm

Parents Address: Shellingford, Farringdon, Berkshire

Military

Enlisted: Marlow

Regiment: Royal Fusiliers (City of London
Regiment) 7 Btn

Rank: Private 68038

Died: Killed in Action 30 October 1917   Aged:38

Place of death:

Buried:

Memorial: Tyne Cot Memorial, Zonnebeke, West
Vlaanderen, Panel 28-30, 162-162A

Additional Information

Formerly Private 242875, 2/5th Queen's R.W. Surrey Regt.

George Gray

Personal

Born: 10/05/1884   in Hambleden

Baptised: 20/07/1884   Hambleden

Occupation: baker

Address: Dryden, Ontario

Family

Married Status: single

Mother: Esther

Father: Charles

Father's occupation: cowman on farm

Parents Address: Pheasant's Hill

Military

Enlisted: Dryden, Ontario

Regiment: Canadian Infantry (Manitoba Reg) 16th 7 Btn

Rank: Private 199086

Died: Killed in Action 08 October 1916   Aged:32

Place of death: Ancre Heights

Buried: Adanac Military Cemetery, Miraumont, Somme, V.E.7

Memorial:

Additional Information

Brother of Harry Gray

Formerly served in 5th Btn Oxon & Bucks Light Infantry.

"Private George Gray, who had been previously reported missing, is now officially reported as killed in action early in October 1916. We offer our sincere sympathy to Mrs. Gray." (South Bucks Press, 05/10/1917)

Harry Gray

Personal

Born: 26/07/1887   in Hambleden
Baptised: 18/09/1887 Hambleden
Occupation: butcher's assistant
Address: living with parents

Family

Married Status: single
Mother: Esther
Father: Charles
Father's occupation: cowman on farm
Parents Address: Pheasant's Hill

Military

Enlisted: Dryden, Ontario
Regiment: Canadian Infantry (Manitoba Reg) 52 Btn
Rank: Private 438765
Died: Died of   10 October 1916   Aged:29
Place of death: Rouen
Buried: St Sever Cemetery, Rouen, B.16.4
Memorial:

Additional Information

"Everybody will deeply sympathise with Mrs. Gray, Pheasants Hill, who has been the recipient of very sad news concerning her soldier sons, Ptes. H. Gray and G. Gray, of the Canadian Forces. They both went to Canada five years ago, but when the call for men came, they answered it. Pte. Harry Gray went to France early last February. On Oct. 9th he addressed a card to his mother from Rouen General Hospital, saying that he was wounded in the left leg. No other news coming to hand, enquiry was made, and it has just been ascertained that he died of his wounds on Oct. 10th. Mrs Gray has also been officially informed that Pte. George Gray is reported missing as from Oct. 8th." (South Bucks Press, 17/11/1916)
Notice of death in Dec 1916 Parish Magazine.

Edmund Higgins

Personal

Born: 19/01/1888   in Pheasants Hill

Baptised: 18/03/1888   Hambleden

Occupation: chair-maker

Address: living with parents

Family

Married Status: single

Mother: Emma

Father: James

Father's occupation: woodman

Parents Address: Little Frieth

Military

Enlisted: High Wycombe

Regiment: Princess Charlotte of Wales's (Royal Berkshire) 6 Btn

Rank: Private 39346

Died: Killed in Action 12 March 1917   Aged:29

Place of death:

Buried:

Memorial: Thiepval Memorial, Somme; Pier & Face 11D

Additional Information

Formerly Private 22928 in the Oxon & Bucks Light Infantry.

"Mr. and Mrs. Higgins, of Little Frieth, have received the sad news that their second son, Pte. E. Higgins (well-known as "Baker"), of the Royal Berks Regiment, has been killed in action. The following letter has been received from a Sergeant in the Regiment: - "Dear Mrs. Higgins, I can't tell you how sorry I am to have to write this letter to you to break the sad news to you of your son's death. He was killed in action on 13th. I can't tell you how sorry I am to lose him as he was such a splendid man. It was his first time in action with this Battalion and he was in my Platoon, and with me at the time of his death. I cannot tell you at present where he was killed by shrapnel, but I can assure you he had as good a burial as possible under the circumstances. Please accept my deepest sympathy." - This gallant soldier, who was 28 years of age, was called to the Colours last April, and after his training went to France, where he was wounded last Autumn, and sent home. He went back to France in Feb. He was a regular player in the Frieth C.C. and the Lane End F.C., and was a good sportsman, of genial disposition, and well-liked by all...."
(South Bucks Press, 06/04/1917)

Notice of Death in the April 1917 Parish Magazine.

John Holland

Personal
  Born: Jan-Mar 1885 in Portobello, Shirburn, Oxon
  Baptised:
  Occupation: Gardener
  Address: Stonor Farm, Henley

Family
  Married Status: married: Bertha C J Holland, Oct-Dec 1904
  Mother: Fanny
  Father: Joseph
  Father's occupation: woodman
  Parents Address: Christmas Common

Military
  Enlisted: High Wycombe
  Regiment: Oxon & Bucks Light Infantry 1/4th Btn
  Rank: Private 202602
  Died: Died of Wounds 20 June 1918   Aged:33
  Place of death: Canove, Italy
  Buried: Montecchio Precalcino Communal
                           Cemetery Extension, Plot 5 Row A Grave 5
  Memorial:

Additional Information
Wounded 15/06/18, died 20/6/18, age 32.
Wounded in attack by Austrian Army near Canove, on first day of the battle of the Piave River.

At time of his death, his wife was living at Christmas Common.
No apparent connection with Hambleden.

Bertram Honeysett

Personal

Born: Jan-Mar 1891   in East Dulwich, London
Baptised:
Occupation: GPO sorting Clerk and Telegraphist
Address: 25 Horse Fair, Banbury

Family

Married Status: married: Winifred Nelly Kilby, Jul-Sep in
                     Banbury
Mother: Miriam Mary
Father: Charles Henry
Father's occupation: Hambleden Postmaster (1897)
Parents Address: 34 St. Marks Road, Henley (1911)

Military

Enlisted: Banbury
Regiment: Corps of Royal Engineers (Signaller)
Rank: Corporal 27316
Died: Died   08 September 1918   Aged:27
Place of death:
Buried: Charmes Military Cemetery, Essegney,
                     Grave I.F.6.
Memorial:

Additional Information

Assumed to have attended Hambleden school when father ran the
Post Office.

George Hopper

Personal
Born: Jan-Mar 1887 in Bexhill, Sussex
Baptised:
Occupation: Water Works Engineer
Address: living with parents

Family
Married Status: married: Alice Hopper of Hambleden
Mother: Margaret
Father: George William
Father's occupation: Insurance Agent
Parents Address: 34 Preston Road, Sidley, Bexhill-on-Sea

Military
Enlisted:
Regiment: Machine Gun Corps (Infantry) 26th Coy.
Rank: Lance Serjeant 12831
Died: Died   18 October 1916   Aged:29
Place of death:
Buried: Warlencourt British Cemetery, Pas de
                     Calais, VI.F.7
Memorial:

Additional Information
Formerly 1057 in Royal Sussex Regiment

George Howson

Personal

Born: 7 Sept 1886 in Overton-on-Dee, Flintshire.

Baptised:

Occupation: Rubber planter, soldier, philanthropist

Address: The Hyde, Hambleden and
                                Kensington

Family

Married Status: Married Jessie Gibson of Victoria, Australia,
                                September 1918

Mother: Ethel

Father: George John Howson

Father's occupation: Clergyman. Archdeacon and Canon
                                Emeritus of Liverpool Cathedral

Parents Address: Overton-on-Dee, later Liverpool

Military

Enlisted: Sept 1914

Regiment: Hampshire Regiment

Rank: Major

Died: Cancer of the pancreas. 28 Nov 1936   Aged: 50

Place of death: South Kensington

Buried: Hambleden New Churchyard, LHS of path

Memorial:

Additional Information

George Howson was awarded the Military Cross in the Battle of Passchen-daele, 1917. He left the army in 1920, and became the founding Chairman of the Disabled Society. In 1922, he suggested to the British Legion – in its infancy then – that the Society should make remembrance poppies for them to sell. With disabled war veteran MP Jack Cohen, he set up a factory on the Old Kent Road in London where five disabled ex-Servicemen began making poppies. Three years later the Poppy Factory moved to its current site in Richmond, Surrey and today produces millions of poppies each year.

His name was added to the Roll of Honour in the Church on his death. It is not on the War Memorial.

Frederick Janes

Personal

Born: Apr-Jun 1898 in Spurgrove, Frieth

Baptised:

Occupation: schoolboy

Address: living with parents

Family

Married Status: single

Mother: Emily

Father: William

Father's occupation: chair-maker

Parents Address: Spurgrove, Frieth

Military

Enlisted: High Wycombe

Regiment: Oxon & Bucks Light Infantry 1/4 Btn, "D Coy

Rank: Private 202740

Died: Killed in Action 16 August 1917   Aged:19

Place of death: Langemarck, during the 3rd Battle of Ypres

Buried:

Memorial: Tyne Cot Memorial, Zonnebeke, West
                                       Vlaanderen, Panel 96-98

Additional Information

The Parish Magazine for Oct 1917 states that the Captain of the Regimer
in which he was serving reported he was shot by a sniper and added tha
"he was a brave boy and did not fear going up to the line although h
realised the danger there was"

Charles Leaver

Personal

Born: 03/07/1898   in Frieth

Baptised:

Occupation: schoolboy

Address: living with parents

Family

Married Status: single

Mother: Sarah

Father: Owen

Father's occupation: carter on farm

Parents Address: Shogmore Cottage, Frieth

Military

Enlisted: High Wycombe

Regiment: Princess Charlotte of Wales's (Royal
                   Berkshire) 1st Btn

Rank: Private 38129

Died: Killed in Action 25 March 1918   Aged:19

Place of death: Arras

Buried: Faubourg-d'Amiens Cemetery, Arras, Pas
                   de Calais, Bay 7

Memorial: Arras Memorial, Faubourg-d'Amiens
                   Cemetery, Pas de Calais

Additional Information

Notice of death in the Parish Magazine for May 1918.

Frederick Leaver

Personal

Born: 20/11/1887	in Frieth
Baptised: 15/01/1888	Hambleden
Occupation:	Grocer's Assistant
Address:	Ealing

Family

Married Status:	married
Mother:	Rebecca
Father:	James
Father's occupation:	publican (Beer retailer) & builder
Parents Address:	The Yew Tree, Frieth

Military

Enlisted:	Ealing
Regiment:	Royal West Surrey (The Queens) 7 Btn
Rank:	Private G/13635
Died: Killed in Action	10 August 1917 Aged:30
Place of death:	Ypres
Buried:	
Memorial:	Ypres (Menin Gate) Memorial, Ieper, Panel 11-13 & 14

Additional Information

The Parish Magazine for Oct 1917 states that Frederick Leaver was killed in action on August 10th - his CO wrote 'he was a good soldier & loved by all his comrades'. "Mr. and Mrs. Leaver, "The Yew Tree", Frieth, have had the sad news of their son Fred's death, in action, on August 10th. He was a Signaller in the Queen's West Surrey Regiment, and up to the time of joining he had resided at Ealing. At one time he was an assistant to Messrs. Holland, Barrett, and Housden, of High Wycombe. He was 29 years of age, and was well liked by everyone who knew him. Our readers will sympathise with the young wife, parents, and relatives of this gallant soldier, who has given his life for King and country. Mrs Leaver has received the following letter: - "Dear Madam, It is with deep regret that I have to inform you of the death of your husband, No. 13635 Pte. F.J. Leaver, who was killed in action on the 10th day of August while in an attack. It may be a little consolation to you, madam, to know that he was a good soldier, and loved by all his comrades, and his loss is greatly felt. I saw him personally before his Company departed from the trenches and his spirit was fine, although he knew only too well what a struggle it was going to be.... I am, yours sincerely, F.W. Webb, C.-Q..-M.-S." (South Bucks Press, 31/08/1917)

Ernest Lyford

Personal

Born: Oct-Dec 1877   in Swyncombe, Oxon

Baptised:

Occupation: agricultural labourer

Address: Moor End

Family

Married Status: single

Mother: Margaret

Father: George

Father's occupation: shepherd

Parents Address: Moor End

Military

Enlisted: High Wycombe

Regiment: Oxon & Bucks Light Infantry 1/4th Btn

Rank: Private 15930

Died: Killed in Action 16 August 1917   Aged:39

Place of death: Langemarck, during 3rd battle of Ypres

Buried:

Memorial: Tyne Cot Memorial, Zonnebeke, West
                           Vlaanderen, Panel 96-98

Additional Information

Notice of death in the Parish Magazine for Sep & Oct 1917.

James McCarter

Personal

Born: Jan-Mar 1885 in Marylebone, Middlesex

Baptised:

Occupation: domestic servant

Address:

Family

Married Status: single

Mother: Mary Ann

Father: James

Father's occupation: police constable

Parents Address: 19 Wimpole St, London (1891)

Military

Enlisted: High Wycombe

Regiment: Coldstream Guards 1st Btn

Rank: Private 18166

Died: Died of Wounds 12 November 1918   Aged:33

Place of death:

Buried: Solesmes British Cemetery, I.A.19

Memorial:

Additional Information

Believed to have been a servant at the Manor House.

The 1911 Census shows him as footman to Henry Seymour Trower at 9 Bryanston Square, London

The South Bucks Press, of 1 Dec 1916, mentions that Pte. McCarter is home (in Hambleden) on leave.

Arthur Miles

Personal
Born: Oct-Dec 1887   in Broad Town, Swindon
Baptised:
Occupation: farm boy
Address: Coombe Terrace, Hambleden

Family
Married Status: married: Emily Franklin at Cricklade
                         Oct-Dec 1908
Mother: Emma Maria
Father: George Tuck
Father's occupation: carter on farm
Parents Address: Swindon, Wiltshire

Military
Enlisted: Oxford
Regiment: Royal Engineers 611th Fortress Coy
Rank: 2nd Corporal 37406
Died: Died at home   31 October 1918   Aged:31
Place of death: Seaforth Hospital, Liverpool
Buried: Bootle Cemetery, Lancs, I.C.E.482
Memorial:

Additional Information
"It is our sad duty this week to record the death of Cpl. Arthur Miles.
The gallant soldier enlisted in the Royal Engineers in June 1915, and
went to France in January of the following year. Five months later
he was wounded in action and on his recovery he was retained
for service in England. He died last week after a short illness from
pneumonia, following influenza, at Seaforth Hospital, Liverpool,
and was buried in the military section of St. Mary's Cemetery, about
a mile from the Hospital, the funeral taking place on Monday last.
The oak coffin was a gift from the Commanding Officer, who also
provided a carriage for the mourners and sent a very handsome
wreath. Wreaths were also sent by the N.C.O.s. and men of the
Seaforth Battery. The body was conveyed from the hospital on a

gun carriage, preceded by the regimental band, and accompanied by the firing party and buglers. Directly following the gun carriage was the pair horse brougham conveying Mrs. Miles (wife) and Mrs. Miles (mother) and a nurse from the hospital. Directly after, three officers walked as chief mourners. Full military honours were accorded. The service was conducted by the senior chaplain, the Rev. Col. Baynes. Everything testified to the very high esteem in which Cpl. Miles was held, and the desire of his officers and comrades to show their appreciation of a soldier's services to his country... The gallant corporal was well known in Hambleden, where he resided for several years before the outbreak of war. He was a well-known figure on the local cricket and football fields, and in this connection had many friends." (South Bucks Press, 08/11/1918)

Brian Molloy

Personal

    Born: Jan-Mar 1876 in Kensington, London

    Baptised:

    Occupation: (Independent means)

    Address: Mayfair, London

Family

    Married Status: married: Gwendoline Beatrice
                                Sanchia May Markham (1910)

    Mother: Florence Emma

    Father: James Lynam

    Father's occupation: barrister; song composer

    Parents Address: Woolleys, Hambleden

Military

    Enlisted:

    Regiment: Queen's Own Oxford Hussars 20 Btn

    Rank: Captain

    Died: Killed in Action 01 November 1914   Aged:38

    Place of death: Messines Ridge

    Buried:

    Memorial: Ypres (Menin Gate) Memorial, Ieper, Panel 5

Additional Information

See main text.

Frederick Plumridge

Personal

Born: 16/10/1886   in The Hyde, Hambleden
Baptised: 05/12/1886   Hambleden
Occupation: farm labourer
Address: The Pheasant Inn, Hambleden

Family

Married Status: single
Mother: Jane
Father: William
Father's occupation: Labourer
Parents Address: Elm Side, Parmoor

Military

Enlisted: High Wycombe
Regiment: Royal Warwickshire 2nd Btn
Rank: Private 29986
Died: Killed in Action 04 October 1917   Aged:30
Place of death: Battle of Broodseinde near Ypres
Buried:
Memorial: Tyne Cot Memorial, Zonnebeke, West
                        Vlaanderen, Panel 23-28 & 163A

Additional Information

Formerly Private 22938 in the Oxon & Bucks Light Infantry
"Official news has been received that 29986 Private F. Plumridge, Royal Warwickshire Regiment, was killed in France on October 4th. The deceased was the third son of the late Mrs. J. Plumridge, of Elm Side, Parmoor, who died last month. He was employed on Lord Parmoor's estate, when he answered the call on April 5th, 1916, and was greatly like in the village and highly esteemed by his employer." (South Bucks Press, 09/11/1917)

"Frederick Plumridge (Pheasants) has been killed in France R.I.P. The following are the brave words of a mother who has lost both her sons, and is left alone in the world " Yes the sacrifice was a willing one : both joined up in 1914. I was proud to let them go." (Parish Magazine, Dec 1917)

It is unclear which of the other sons died in the War – no other Plumridge is recorded on local war memorials.

Arthur Richardson

Personal

Born: 14/07/1886   in Hambleden

Baptised: 05/09/1886 Hambleden

Occupation: Post Office worker

Address: 58 Charteris Road Kilburn

Family

Married Status: married: Marjorie Dorothy Tompkins on 1/8/1915 at Medmenham

Mother: Sofia

Father: Richard

Father's occupation: cowman

Parents Address: Workhouse Yard, Hambleden

Military

Enlisted: Oxford, 29/05/1915

Regiment: Kings Royal Rifle Corps 2nd Btn

Rank: Rifleman R/11373

Died: Killed in Action 29 April 1916   Aged: 29

Place of death: Ypres

Buried: Maroc British Cemetery, Grenay, Pas de Calais, I.A.10

Memorial:

Additional Information

"The news reached Hambleden on Sunday morning of the death of Rifleman A. Richardson, who was killed in action on Saturday, April 29th. The gallant soldier was well known in the village, of which he was a native... Before entering the Army last year, Rifleman Richardson was employed at the Post Office, and was also caretaker at the Institute. Here deep regret will be felt at the death of "Nat", as he was popularly named, who, besides being an excellent custodian, was also a popular member. The news came to the village by means of a letter from his officer, addressed to the late soldier's sister, Mrs. Watson, - It is with great regret that I write to you, as

Rifleman Richardson's sister, to tell you how sorry I am at losing him. He was a most useful man on a Lewis gun. His death on the 29th April was instantaneous, and a Captain and four other riflemen were killed by the same aerial torpedo. He is buried in a little cemetery in a village behind the firing line. A wooden cross and grass and flowers are on his grave... Yours sincerely, 2nd LIEUT. P.D. Ravenscoft, 2nd K.R.R.C." (South Bucks Press, 12/05/1916)

Frederick Rixon

Personal

Born: Oct-Dec 1884 in Burnham, Bucks

Baptised:

Occupation: Domestic gardener

Address: Hambleden

Family

Married Status: married: Annie Gough, Apr-Jun 1909 in Midhurst

Mother: Charlotte

Father: Frank

Father's occupation: Labourer

Parents Address: Burnham (1881)

Military

Enlisted: Reading

Regiment: Princess Charlotte of Wales's (Royal Berks Regiment), 7th Btn.

Rank: Private 19413

Died: Killed in Action 24 April 1917   Aged:32

Place of death: Battle of Doiran, Balkan Front, Macedonia

Buried:

Memorial: Doiran Memorial

Additional Information

Brought up by his uncle Fred Rixon in Henley

Alfred Rose

Personal

Born: Apr-Jun 1886 in Haddenham, Bucks

Baptised:

Occupation: Insurance Collector [BR: labourer on farm]

Address: Chalfont St Peter

Family

Married Status: married: Myrtle Alean Hobbs (formerly Rose) née Morhen, 5/10/1906 at Hambleden

Mother: Edith

Father: George

Father's occupation: Hay binder

Parents Address: Haddenham

Military

Enlisted: Marlow

Regiment: Hampshire Regiment 2nd Btn

Rank: Lance Corporal 38456

Died: Died of Wounds 28 November 1917   Aged:31

Place of death: Cambrai

Buried:

Memorial: Cambrai Memorial, Louverval, Nord, Panel 7

Additional Information

The Parish Magazine for Jan 1907 lists the marriage to Myrtle Alean Morhen on Dec 5th 1906.

The Parish Magazine for Jan 1918 states: "...died of wounds in France in the Field Ambulance on November 28th R.I.P."

Henry Sherlock

Personal

Born: Oct-Dec 1889 in Hambleden
Baptised:
Occupation: Mechanical Engineer
Address: Farnborough, Hants

Family

Married Status: single
Mother: Hannah
Father: Francis
Father's occupation: licenced victualler
Parents Address: 34 St Andrews Rd, Henley (in 1901,
                     the parents were living at the Stag Inn,
                     Hambleden)

Military

Enlisted: High Wycombe
Regiment: Royal Army Ordnance Corps; attchd. Ox &
                     Bucks LI 1st Btn
Rank: Staff Sergeant (Armourer) A/2773
Died: Died of Wounds 10 November 1917   Aged:28
Place of death: Mesopotamia
Buried: Baghdad (North Gate) War Cemetery, IX.D.9
Memorial:

Additional Information

"It is with regret that we announce the death of Armr.-S.-Sergt. H.
Sherlock, who, as we reported in our last issue, was taken ill with
cholera while serving with the Forces in Mesopotamia. Sergt. Sherlock
had made rapid progress in the profession of arms since he enlisted in
the Army Ordnance Corps, and in a very short time rose to the position
he occupied at the time of his death. He was very well known in the
village and district, and had made many friends..." (South Bucks Press,
23/11/1917)

"Our readers will be interested in the following letter which has been received by the parents of the late S.-Sergeant Sherlock, who died of cholera on Nov. 10th while serving with the Forces in Mesopotamia: - "I am writing to give you particulars of the death of your son, on Nov. 10th. About a fortnight ago he broke his glasses, and went into Baghdad to get a second pair from his dump kit. Whilst there he must have been infected by cholera, for on returning here he developed the disease. The doctors told me that on Thursday, Nov. 7th, he was almost out of danger, but on Friday he had a serious relapse. He was buried by the Regiment. A capable man, keen on his work, he was a credit to the Regiment... Yours sincerely, G. Whittall, Lt.-Col., Oxford and Bucks Lt. Infantry." (South Bucks Press, 18/01/1918)

Harry Silvester

Personal

Born: Oct-Dec 1887   in Hambleden

Baptised:

Occupation:

Address: 87th Street, Edmonton, Alberta

Family

Married Status: married: Elizabeth (last address Elm
                         Creek, Manitoba)

Mother: Thirza

Father: Job Townsend

Father's occupation: carpenter on estate

Parents Address: Greenlands

Military

Enlisted: Edmonton, Canada 16 Apr 1915

Regiment: Canadian Infantry (Central Ontario
                         Regiment) 15 Btn,

Rank: Private 437071

Died: 01 September 1918   Aged:30

Place of death:

Buried: Dominion Cemetery, Hendecourt les
                         Cagnicourt, Pas de Calais.

Memorial:

Additional Information

Formerly in 101st Regiment, Canadian Infantry

Embarkation 1st April 1916 from Halifax on S.S. Olympic

Valentine Silvester

Personal

Born: 14/02/1899   in Hambleden

Baptised: 16/03/1899   Hambleden

Occupation: schoolboy

Address: living with parents

Family

Married Status: single

Mother: Thirza

Father: Job Townsend

Father's occupation: carpenter on estate

Parents Address: Greenlands

Military

Enlisted: High Wycombe

Regiment: Gloucestershire 8 Btn

Rank: Private 39384

Died: Died   18 April 1918   Aged:19

Place of death: Belgium

Buried:

Memorial: Tyne Cot Memorial, Zonnebeke, West Vlaanderen, Panel 72-75

Additional Information

Formerly Private 31140 in the Oxon & Bucks Light Infantry

"We regret to learn that Pte. V. Silvester, Gloucester Regt., is officially reported missing. Pte. Silvester is the youngest of five brothers (sons of Mr. and Mrs. Silvester, Dairy-lane, Greenlands), who are serving with the Forces. Enlisting in the Royal Bucks Hussars, he was transferred to the Gloucesters after arrival in France..." (South Bucks Press, 31/05/1918)

The Parish Magazine for Oct 1918 states "reported missing after a very brief service in France and is now supposed to have been killed."

William Smith

Personal

Born: 25/11/1874   in Hambleden
Baptised: 10/01/1875 Hambleden
Occupation: soldier
Address: Murrumburrah, New South Wales

Family

Married Status: married: Constance May Smith (last
                address Flint Cottage, Frieth)
Mother: Jane
Father: William
Father's occupation: Labourer
Parents Address: Flint Cottage, Frieth

Military

Enlisted: Sydney, NSW, 9/10/1914
Regiment: Australian Imperial Force 1st Btn
Rank: Private 1112
Died: Killed in Action 03 October 1917   Aged:42
Place of death:
Buried:
Memorial: Ypres (Menin Gate) Memorial, Ieper,
                Panel 31

Additional Information

Served in Boer War, 7 years as a soldier.
Age 30 on arrival in New South Wales.
"Much sympathy will be felt for Mrs. Smith, Flint Cottage, Frieth, who has received news of the death, in action, of her husband, Pte. W. Smith, of the Australian Expeditionary Force. The gallant soldier was married on Sept. 13th, and returned to the Front four days later. His officer, writing to his widow, says he was killed in the fighting north of Ypres, on Oct. 4th. Pte. Smith, as the officer's letter indicates, was held in high esteem by the officers and men of his company" (South Bucks Press, 26/10/1917)

153

Walter Stainton

Personal
    Born: in
    Baptised:
    Occupation:
    Address:

Family
    Married Status:
    Mother:
    Father:
    Father's occupation:
    Parents Address:

Military
    Enlisted:
    Regiment:
    Rank:
    Died: Aged:
    Place of death:
    Buried:
    Memorial:

Additional Information

No information about this person has been found.

James Taylor

Personal

    Born: c. 1895   in Bray, Berks

    Baptised:

    Occupation:

    Address:

Family

    Married Status:

    Mother: Emma

    Father: William

    Father's occupation: sub Postmaster & grocer

    Parents Address: Post Office, Tittle Row, Bray

Military

    Enlisted: Oxford

    Regiment: Royal Berkshire 8 Btn

    Rank: Private 16198

    Died: Killed in Action 25 July 1916   Aged:21

    Place of death:

    Buried:

    Memorial: Thiepval Memorial, Somme; Pier & Face 11D

Additional Information

Details have been derived from Buckinghamshire Remembers website but have not been independently verified. No definite link can be found to Hambleden, Frieth or Skirmett.

Ralph Tilbury

Personal

Born: 23/02/1891   in Hambleden

Baptised: 03/05/1891   Hambleden

Occupation: Labourer/Soldier

Address: living at home (1901)

Family

Married Status: married: Phyllis Victoria Caroline Edwards, 22/4/1916 in Hambleden

Mother: Florence

Father: William

Father's occupation: Woodman

Parents Address: Coombe Bottom, Hambleden

Military

Enlisted: Reading

Regiment: Rifle Brigade

Rank: Sergeant 3045

Died: Died at Home   Aged:31

Place of death: At Home

Buried:

Memorial:

Additional Information

Started as Bugler, then Corporal, then Sergeant.

Discharged as no longer physically fit for War Service on 23 August 1916

Died at home, from injuries or disease sustained on active service, Oct-Dec 1922

Ralph Tilbury's name is one of the last names recorded on the Roll of Honour in the Church; it is not on the War Memorial – a reflection of the fact that he died after the War Memorial was erected.

Thomas Trendall

Personal

Born: Jan-Mar 1895   in Marlow

Baptised:

Occupation: Farm Labourer

Address:

Family

Married Status: single

Mother: Sophia Trendall (1901 now married
                              to William Sears)

Father: Thomas Edwin Trendall

Father's occupation: chair maker

Parents Address: Little Frieth (1917), Ditchfield, Marlow
                              (1901), West Wycombe (1891)

Military

Enlisted: Sittingbourne, Kent

Regiment: Queen's (Royal West Surrey) 1st Btn

Rank: Lance Corporal G/21993

Died: Killed in Action 03 March 1917   Aged:22

Place of death: Somme

Buried: Perrone Communal Cemetery Extension,
                              V.N.18

Memorial:

Additional Information

"Last week Mrs. W. Sears, of Little Frieth, received news from the War Office that her son, Corpl. T. Trendall, aged 22 years, the only surviving son of the late Thos. Edmund Trendall, of Lane End, killed in action on Mar. 3. This gallant young soldier had seen much service, having enlisted at the outbreak of War. He trained at Curragh Camp, Ireland, and then proceeded with the 17th Lancers to France in Sept. 1915. He was wounded, and invalided home in January 1916, and remained in England for light duty until December last, when he again proceeded to France, being transferred to the Queen's Royal West Surrey Regiment. This young soldier, whose kind disposition had made many friends among his mates in the Battalion, was loved by all..." (South Bucks Press, 06/04/1917)

Listed in the Hambleden Roll of Honour as Thomas Frendall.

The 1911 Census shows him as an inmate at the Borstal Institute, Rochester (aged 16).

Harry Vivian

Personal

Born: Oct-Dec 1898 in Cornwood, Devon

Baptised:

Occupation: schoolboy

Address: Hambleden

Family

Married Status: single

Mother: Mary

Father: Albert Edward

Father's occupation: farmer

Parents Address: Colstrope Farm, Hambleden

Military

Enlisted: Caversham

Regiment: Worcestershire 3 Btn (& 31420 Ox & Bucks LI)

Rank: Private 57397

Died: Killed in Action 19 October 1918   Aged:19

Place of death:

Buried: Romeries Communal Cemetery Extension, France, III.B.20

Memorial:

Additional Information

Formerly Private 31420 in the Oxon & Bucks Light Infantry

"Feelings of deep regret were aroused in the neighbourhood when it became known that Mr. and Mrs. Vivian, Colstrope Farm, Hambleden, had received news that their only son, Private Harry Vivian, Worcestershire Regiment, had been killed in action. The intimation came in the form of a letter from the gallant lad's officer, who writes: - "I regret to inform you that your son, Pte. Vivian, was killed by a shell on the afternoon of the 19th October. About three weeks ago he was transferred to the Battalion Observers, and since that time he has done excellent work. He was chosen as being the best man in his Company, and I assure you that the

Section has suffered tremendously by his loss. He was killed almost instantaneously, the shell bursting about five yards from him. I thought it might give you a little comfort in your greatest trial to know that he suffered no pain." - Widely known and as widely liked, Harry Vivian will be missed by many. He was a bright, cheerful, and sturdy lad, who made friends wherever he went. While still too young to serve in the Forces, he went to France to work in a civil capacity behind the lines. When age permitted he joined the Oxford Yeomanry, but was later transferred to the Infantry. At the time of his death matters were in train for a commission for him...." (South Bucks Press, 08/11/1918)

Private Vivian died just two weeks before the war ended.

Rowland Webster

Personal

Born: 14/02/1868   in

Baptised:

Occupation:

Address: Hambleden Place

Family

Married Status:

Mother:

Father:

Father's occupation:

Parents Address:

Military

Enlisted:

Regiment: City of London Yeomanry (Rough Riders)

Rank: Captain (retd)

Died: Died at Home   08 March 1915   Aged:47

Place of death: London

Buried: Hambleden New Churchyard, RHS of path

Memorial: Dozinghem Military Cemetery, Poperinge, Belgium, II.A.9

Additional Information

"We regret to record the death of Captain Webster, of Hambleden Place. The death occurred in London on Monday night. The gallant officer, who had seen service in India and Ceylon, came to Hambleden to live only last year. Shortly after the outbreak of the war, he rejoined the Army and became attached to the Army Service Corps, and was stationed at the Curragh. Captain Webster was seized with an attack of pneumonia, to which he succumbed." (South Bucks Press, 12/03/1915) Buried on 11 March 1915 (Parish Magazine, April 1915)

Captain Rowland Valentine Webster was in Colombo, Ceylon in 1911 - when he bought the Nimrod from Sir Ernest Shackleton.

161

Notice in the London Gazette, concerning his estate after death: "Rowland Valentine Webster, late of Hambleden-place, Hambleden, in the county of Bucks, and Colombo, in the Island of Ceylon, deceased, Captain (retired) in His Majesty's Army, and proprietor of the Webster Automatic Packeting Factory, Colombo".

Sidney White

Personal

    Born: Jan-Mar 1881   in Foxcotte, near Andover, Hants

    Baptised:

    Occupation: Laundry Proprietor

    Address: Pheasants Hill

Family

    Married Status: married: Alice Ann Mary (married c. 1906)

    Mother: Elizabeth

    Father: Henry

    Father's occupation: Chair maker

    Parents Address: Foxcotte, near Andover, Hants

Military

    Enlisted: Marlow

    Regiment: Coldstream Guards 3 Btn

    Rank: Private 18473

    Died: Died of Wounds 29 July 1917   Aged:36

    Place of death:

    Buried: Dozinghem Military Cemetery, West-Vlaanderen, Grave   II.A.g.

    Memorial:

Additional Information

"The news that Pte. S. T. White, of Pheasants Hill, had died as the result of wounds received in action was received in the village with feelings of deepest regret. It appears that he was wounded in the fighting on July 29th, and died a few hours afterwards, without recovering consciousness, in the casualty Clearing Hospital. The gallant soldier answered the call to duty when Lord Derby called for recruits to the groups, and when his turn came he joined the Coldstream Guards. Before joining the Army, the late Guardsman was an enthusiastic and able member of the Hambleden Platoon of the Bucks Volunteer Regiment. Mr. White was always ready to take his share in any movement which was calculated to benefit the community in which he lived. A member of the Congregational Church at Pheasants Hill, he took an active part in the work there, and was for some time superintendent of the Sunday School. He was a most useful member of the Committee of both the Men's Institute and the Hambleden Cricket Club. His cheerful disposition and hearty laugh will be missed by the many friends which he made. The deepest sympathy will be felt for his wife and two children." (South Bucks Press, 17/08/1917)

Reginald Willsher

Personal

    Born: 14/01/1892   in Hambleden

    Baptised: 08/05/1892 Hambleden

    Occupation: Gardener

    Address: living with parents

Family

    Married Status: single

    Mother: Mary Ann

    Father: Arthur

    Father's occupation: Coachman/Chauffeur

    Parents Address: Woolleys Cottage, Hambleden

Military

    Enlisted: Oxford

    Regiment: Oxon & Bucks Light Infantry 2nd Btn

    Rank: Corporal 12222

    Died: Killed in Action 13 November 1916   Aged:24

    Place of death: Beaumont-Hamel

    Buried: Redan Ridge Cemetery No.3, Beaumont-Hamel, France, A.20

    Memorial:

Additional Information

Albert Reginald Willsher Baptism record gives surname as Wiltshire

Lads, You're Wanted

'Lads, you're wanted, go and help,'
On the railway carriage wall
Stuck the poster, and I thought
Of the hands that penned the call.

Fat civilians wishing they
'Could go and fight the Hun'.
Can't you see them thanking God
That they're over forty-one?

Girls with feathers, vulgar songs -
Washy verse on England's need -
God - and don't we damned well
know
How the message ought to read

'Lads, you're wanted! over there,'
Shiver in the morning dew,
More poor devils like yourselves
Waiting to be killed by you

Go and help to swell the names
In the casualty lists.
Help to make the column's stuff
For the blasted journalists.

Help to keep them nice and safe
From the wicked German foe.
Don't let him come over here!
Lads, you're wanted - out you go.'

There's a better word than that,
Lads, and can't you hear it come
From a million men that call
You to share their martyrdom?

Leave the harlots still to sing
Comic songs about the Hun,
Leave the fat old men to say
Now *we've* got them on the run.

Better twenty honest years
Than their dull three score and ten.
Lads, you're wanted. Come and
learn
To live and die with honest men.

You shall learn what men can do
If you will but pay the price,
Learn the gaiety and strength
In the gallant sacrifice.

Take your risk of life and death
Underneath the open sky.
Live clean or go out quick -
Lads, you're wanted. Come and die.

Ewart Alan Mackintosh

166

Bibliography

100 Days to Victory : Saul David : Hodder and Stoughton, London, 2013

1913 The Defiant Swan Song : Virginia Cowles : Weidenfeld and Nicholson, London, 1967

1913 The World Before the Great War : Charles Emmerson : Bodley Head, London, 2013

1914 The Days of Hope : Lyn Macdonald : Penguin Books, London 1987

1914-1918 The History of the First World War : David Stevenson : Penguin, London 2012

A History of the Culden Faw Estate : Sally Strutt : Culden Faw, Hambleden 2013

August 1914 : Barbara W. Tuchman : Constable, London, 1962

Born on Chiltern Slopes : Charles Gray : Pheasants Hill Press, Hambleden, 2003.

British Tommy 1914 – 1918 : Pegler and Chappell : Osprey, London, 1996

Buckinghamshire Within Living Memory : BFWI : Countryside Books, Newbury, 1993

Catastrophe - Europe Goes to War 1914 : Max Hastings : William Collins, London, 2013

Europe's Last Summer : David Fromkin : Vintage, London, 2005

Great Britain's Great War : Jeremy Paxman : Viking/Penguin, London, 2013

How the Labourer Lives, A Study of the Rural Labour Problem : Rowntree and Kendall : T. Nelson, London, 1913

Kitchener's Army -The Raising of the New Armies : Peter Simkins : Pen & Sword, Barnsley, 2007

Mud, Blood and Poppycock : Gordon Corrigan : Cassell, London, 2004

On Chiltern Slopes : AH Stanton : Basil Blackwell, Oxford, 1927

Soldiers : Richard Holmes : Harper Press, London, 2012

Somme : Lyn Macdonald : Papermac, Macmillan Publishing, London 1984

The Art of Captaincy : Mike Brearley : Hodder & Stoughton, London 1985

The British Army in World War 1 (Parts 1 & 2) : Mike Chappell : Osprey, Oxford, 2003

The Edwardians : Roy Hattersley : Abacus, London, 2006

The Fateful Year : Mark Bostridge, Viking Penguin, London, 2014

The Last Great War : Adrian Gregory : Cambridge University Press, Cambridge, 2013

The Long Shadow : David Reynolds : Simon & Schuster UK, London, 2013

The Sleepwalkers : Christopher Clark, Penguin Books, London 2013

The War That Ended Peace : Margaret MacMillan : Profile Books, London, 2013

Tommy : Richard Holmes : Harper Collins, London, 2004

http://www.leamarsh.com/marshlane/villiers.html

http://www.friethhistory.org.html